HOW TO IMPROVE YOUR MARKETING COPY

Ian Linton

KOGAN PAGE

First published in 1993

Apart from any fair dealing for the purposes of research or private study, or criticism or review, as permitted under the Copyright, Designs and Patents Act, 1988, this publication may only be reproduced, stored or transmitted, in any form or by any means, with the prior permission in writing of the publishers, or in the case of reprographic reproduction in accordance with the terms of licences issued by the Copyright Licensing Agency. Enquiries concerning reproduction outside those terms should be sent to the publishers at the undermentioned address:

Kogan Page Limited
120 Pentonville Road
London N1 9JN

© Ian Linton, 1993

British Library Cataloguing in Publication Data

A CIP record for this book is available from the British Library.

ISBN 0 7494 0891 X

Typeset by DP Photosetting, Aylesbury, Bucks
Printed and bound in Great Britain by
Biddles Ltd, Guildford and King's Lynn

HOW TO IMPROVE YOUR MARKETING COPY

CONTENTS

●●

PART 1   IMPROVING YOUR MARKETING COPY

1   Introduction   11
Aims of the book   11
An outline of the book   13

2   The scope of marketing copy   17
The importance of good copywriting   17
Approaches to copywriting   19
Publications describing products   20
Publications that help develop market share   23
Publications describing a company   25
Summary   26

3   Setting communications tasks   27
Business objectives   27
Marketing objectives   27
Communications objectives   28
Summary   30

4   The target audience   31
Analysing a target audience   31
Decision-making groups   31
Project teams   34
Targeting the audience – an overview   38
How targeting changes with different purchasing situations   40
Summary   44

5   Using research   46

6   Planning perceptions   48
Perception varies by audience   48
Relating perceptions to research findings   48
Building planned perceptions into copy   49
Relating perceptions to your own strengths   50
Reflecting customers' needs   50

6 / Contents

Changing established perceptions   50
Examples of planned perceptions   52
Summary   54

7 Auditing copy   56
Background   56
Scope of the audit   56
Auditing internal awareness of key issues   57
Auditing consistent presentation of key messages   58
Auditing effective support of customer relations   58
Summary   59

8 Language   60
The language of quality   60
The language of customer care   61
The language of business technology   64
Summary   66

9 Developing key messages   67
Example 1: Lawn-mowers   67
Example 2: Computers   68
Example 3: Furniture   71
Example 4: Accountancy services   72
Example 5: Business credit cards   73
Example 6: Training services   74
Example 7: Video cameras   75
Example 8: Leisure centres   76
Example 9: Industrial materials   77
Example 10: Business telephones   78
Building key messages into copy   79
Summary   80

10 Planning copy content   81
Helping other people to evaluate your work   81
Structuring a contents list   81
Examples of copy content   82
Summary   85

11 The copy brief   86
Background   86
Objectives   86
Competitive information   87
Product information   87

Target audience   87
Target perception   88
Mechanical information   88
Approval of the brief   88
An example of a brief   88
Summary   90

PART 2   WRITING TASKS

12   Writing about products   93
Launching a new product to the salesforce   93
Launching an innovative product   96
Adding value to commodity products   99
Branding high value products   101
Making consumer technology simple   105
Marketing training services   108

13   Writing about market development   112
Dealing with a new market opportunity   112
Appealing to different segments of the market   115
Helping customers to use your products   117
Building understanding of services   119
Overcoming salesforce resistance   122
Building customer loyalty through dealerships   124
Selling a sales programme to retailers   128

14   Writing about companies   131
Demonstrating company capability   131
Describing professional service capability   134
Repositioning a company to enter a new market   137
Recruiting good people   140
Building confidence in investors   143
Explaining a changing business to investors   145

Index   *150*

Part
ONE

IMPROVING YOUR MARKETING COPY

Chapter ONE

INTRODUCTION

Good writing is an essential part of the marketing communications process. It persuades people to buy your products, reassures them that you're a good company to do business with, helps them make decisions about your products and services and makes them feel that you care about your customers. The copy in a sales leaflet or a proposal document takes the place of a persuasive sales representative long after the presentation. It acts on your behalf when a group of customers are talking about your products and services and it helps them make decisions about you.

For all its importance, copywriting is a neglected area. The glamorous end of copywriting – advertisements and commercials – is always handled by a professional but, when it comes down to business presentations or sales literature, anyone with a remote interest in the subject is happy to have a go at the copy. After all, 'Anyone can write, it's what we did at school.' Multinational corporations refuse to credit copywriters on product brochures in which they will happily acknowledge designers, printers and photographers, because 'We wouldn't want customers to think that we couldn't write our own copy.'

All of this implies that marketing copy is fair game for anyone; there's no special skill required and there's no reason why any company should want to use a professional writer. But apply the same argument to finance – 'I've got a bank account and I do the household budgets' – or sales – 'I can use a telephone and I've raised a bit of money for charity' – and the argument begins to look suspect. Any company that wants to remain competitive and improve its market position looks closely at the effectiveness of all its skills.

AIMS OF THE BOOK

The book aims to show you how to:

- improve the quality and effectiveness of copy in marketing publications and presentations;
- plan and produce effective copy;

- understand the information requirements of different members of the target audience;
- use research to develop key messages and target perceptions;
- brief professional writers;
- evaluate the work of other writers;
- understand the copy requirements of key business issues such as partnership, customer focus and customer loyalty.

Improving the quality of copy

This is an aim that affects everyone involved in writing – those who commission and those who write. Publications have to work hard because they have a role to play in the marketing communications process. This book will define the role that each publication and presentation plays and will show how the copy is shaped by that role. The copy must work as hard as the design or photographs to improve communications between an organization and its customers.

Planning and producing copy

Getting down to practicalities, the book will provide you with a step-by-step guide to commissioning or writing good copy. It shows how research and understanding of business are vital to effective writing, and it shows the key stages in planning.

Understanding information requirements

Good copy does not exist in a vacuum. It provides readers or customers with the information they need to make decisions about your products or services. This book explains the ways in which purchasing decisions are made and explains how to find out what people look for in a product or service. That way your copy will be focused on what the reader needs to know and you will be making it easy to buy. It also explains how different members of the target audience have different information needs. When a board director, departmental manager and technical specialist are all involved in the purchasing decision, it's important that each one gets the right message.

Using research

Research can be the writer's most valuable asset. When you know how and why customers buy specific products and why they prefer some companies, you're in a strong position to get the message right. Provided your product or service meets those requirements, you will be able to present relevant compelling messages.

Briefing professional writers

You may not have the skills to tackle every type of writing yourself. This book explains how to develop a copy brief and shows all the important information that should be included in it. In this way you will be able to get the best results from a professional writer and the best value for money.

Evaluating the work of other writers

When you're looking at writing produced by other people you need to know how to evaluate it. It isn't sufficient to say it doesn't flow or it lacks punch. You need to provide clear objective comments that the writer can use to improve the final result. The best results are achieved when the writer and the commissioner work in partnership. The book shows you how to achieve that kind of relationship.

Understanding key business issues

Copy doesn't just describe products and services. It helps to achieve business objectives and, in the modern business environment, the key issues are partnership, customer focus and customer loyalty. This book explains how these issues can be integrated into every aspect of copy.

AN OUTLINE OF THE BOOK

Scope of copywriting

This section looks at the main types of business communication, analysing the contribution the publication makes to the whole communications process and the type of writing that is needed to make that publication work. You will be able to understand the importance of writing each of these publications properly and you will ensure that each gets the proper attention. Each publication has an important role to play in getting the commitment of people and in building understanding in customers and prospects.

Communications tasks

Copy is not written in isolation; it does not just describe a product or service, or support the pictures. Copywriting is an integral part of the marketing communications process and the writer must understand the role of marketing. He must begin by understanding the overall business objectives – where the company is going, what it wants to achieve. These translate into marketing objectives, to achieve a 10 per cent market share, for example. Communications tasks support marketing objectives, for example to persuade 200 prospects that the product will provide them with definite benefits. This section explains the methods of identifying communications tasks from marketing objectives and gives a number of practical examples.

Target audience

Copywriters don't write for the general public. They prepare messages that are targeted at specific groups of people. Their task is to convey a clear message to someone who has been identified as the main buyer or influence in the purchasing decision. In consumer copywriting, the reader and the buyer are often the same person, but in industrial or business purchasing the situation becomes more complex. The writer needs to understand how companies buy products – what is the role of the purchasing officer, technical manager, chief executive, departmental manager or marketing executive? What do each of these contribute to the purchase decision? This section has a number of examples to show decision making and purchasing in consumer and business situations and shows how you can develop a plan for identifying and preparing messages that are precisely focused on your audience.

Using research

Closely related to audience research is research into the market. Why do people buy products and services? Why do they prefer some products to others? What are the most important factors they consider when they are choosing a product? How do the company's products and services compare with their competitors'? This is the kind of information that research can provide and it is invaluable in helping the writer to develop a copy approach for a product or service. This section identifies research sources and shows how to use the information to develop copy approaches.

Planning perceptions

This allows you to manage the way companies, products and services are perceived. For example, a computer maintenance company knew that its services were regarded as essential but not strategic. It wanted to become a strategic supplier at a much higher level, so it developed a planned perception of the company as a business partner. To achieve this meant building a planned perception over a period of time and ensuring that all the communications supported this. This section shows how to achieve that. It shows how the planned perception is based on research and can be achieved by the consistent use of key messages. The section also gives examples of planned perceptions for a number of different products and services.

Auditing

This is a technique for finding out how current and planned copy is actually working. An audit looks at both publications and people – analysing the content of publications and looking at the way people view the company or product to see whether the planned perceptions are actually being achieved. The section gives a step by step guide to conducting an audit and shows that it should be carried out regularly for the most effective results.

Language of copywriting

Language is only a small part of the whole writing process. It is far more important that the writer understands what he is trying to achieve, who he is communicating with, what the intended result is, and why it is important. Only when this is understood, does language become important. This section shows how language varies from one product to another.

Developing key messages

Key messages should be included in every form of communication and they should be used consistently over a long period of time. This section takes a wide range of products and services and shows the key messages that should be incorporated. The key messages provide the vital link between different forms of communication, but they should not obstruct product and service messages. Key messages vary from product to product and they also vary according to the target audience. The section takes each product from a different perspective and helps you to recognize the differences.

Planning copy content

This section takes a number of different products and services and shows how to plan the copy for each one. The planning begins with the key positioning statements that must be built into every communication. It then looks at the individual products or services that describe them and shows how to analyse the main communications requirements. What do people need to know to buy this product or service? How can it be best presented?

Briefing a project

A writing project should always begin with a proper brief. This includes the marketing objectives, the target audience, the intended results and the media that have been selected. This section shows the detailed information that a writer needs to have so that he can produce the best possible results. It shows the level of background – why the project is important, what the current problems in the market are, and what the copy has to achieve. It analyses the target market and shows how it can be broken down into smaller segments, each with their own specific concerns. It looks at the product or service in detail showing the main features and benefits and how these relate to the concerns of the target audience. It highlights any research available and shows how this has led to target perceptions and to the key messages that should be communicated. It describes the media and the results that are intended. A number of examples, together with a step-by-step guide, show the writer how to prepare and conclude a brief. These also show how to evaluate copy results.

Writing tasks

This section brings together the different strands of the book. It takes a wide range of communications tasks and shows how research, planned perceptions, audience research and many other factors influence the shape of the copy. It provides practical examples of copy for each of the following marketing activities:

- Writing about products:
  - launching a new product to the salesforce;
  - launching innovative products;
  - adding value to commodity products;
  - branding high value products;
  - making consumer technology simple;
  - marketing management training.

- Writing about market development:
  - dealing with new market opportunities;
  - appealing to different segments of the market;
  - helping customers use your products;
  - building understanding of services;
  - overcoming salesforce resistance;
  - building customer loyalty through dealerships;
  - selling a sales programme to retailers.

- Writing about companies:
  - demonstrating company capability;
  - demonstrating service capability;
  - repositioning a company to enter new markets;
  - recruiting good people;
  - building confidence in investors;
  - explaining a changing business to investors.

Chapter TWO

THE SCOPE OF MARKETING COPY

This chapter describes the different types of marketing publication and explains why it is important that they are well written. It also explains different approaches to copywriting.

The publications are divided into three groups:

1. Publications describing products
   - leaflets
   - catalogues
   - product brochures
   - data sheets
   - product guides
   - technical updates.

2. Publications that help to develop market share
   - management guides
   - executive brochures
   - sales guides
   - salesforce communications
   - dealer communications.

3. Publications describing a company
   - corporate brochures.

Each type of publication has a different role to play in raising awareness or persuading the customer to buy a product or service.

THE IMPORTANCE OF GOOD COPYWRITING

Making it easier for customers to buy products

Copy makes it easier for customers to buy your products – why put barriers in their way? Make sure they understand how your products will benefit them and make sure they know which product is right for them. If they're confused, they'll turn to a company with a simpler product range and clearer information.

Here is an example of some helpful copy from a computer services company.

It's taken from a customer guide to the services available. It begins with an informative headline:

> Supporting all your products in a multi-vendor environment.

The phrases 'all your products' and 'multi-vendor' signal to the reader, if this is your problem, read on. That's an ideal way to catch someone who's flicking through a brochure for the first time. The headline is followed by a scenario that outlines what the supplier knows about the customer's business.

> You have invested in products from a number of different manufacturers and you need to provide a consistent level of support across your whole installation.

The customer relates to that immediately – a supplier who understands my problem, a company that focuses on my needs, instead of selling me something I don't need. What are they actually offering? You've got the reader's interest, now go for the sale.

> We have developed the capability to provide our support in various forms, including systems integration, managed networks, managed service or facilities management. We are committed to Open Systems and the range of non-ABC products we support is already wider than the ABC range.

That's a simple statement of what the company can offer and, just in case the customer wants a simple summary, there is a simple checklist headed 'Relevant services' with bullet points listing the main services. All the elements are there to help the customer understand and buy your product. It also makes it easier for your sales people to sell your products.

Building understanding of a company

Good copy also builds understanding of your company. That's important because customers need reassuring that they can do business with you. You won't let them down and you'll keep developing products and services that benefit their business. This credit card processing company leaves its customers in no doubts about their future relationship.

> Our strategic business objective is to maintain our position as Europe's leading independent card processor and develop further added-value services for our clients.

They're not just heading in a direction that suits *their* needs, they're going to help their *customers* improve the performance of their own business.

> So that you benefit directly from these developments, we will keep you informed of our plans and hold regular review meetings.

The customer can see real value in doing business with this company.

> By working together, we will continue to meet your changing business needs.

The approach could be even simpler. When a car manufacturer is looking for new distributors, it offers them a powerful business proposition – join the market leaders and share in our success.

> As a prospective dealer you could be working in partnership with one of the world's most successful car makers. In Europe, more than one in ten of all vehicles on the road are manufactured by us. We have achieved this dominant share of the market through a combination of high-quality, well-equipped, value-for-money products, backed by convenient comprehensive after-sales service. To help build dealership business, we provide market-leading products backed by comprehensive training, marketing and business support.

That distributor knows exactly what sort of company he will be working with.

APPROACHES TO COPYWRITING

If writing is so important, how should it be handled? In most businesses, there are four approaches to writing:

1. The do-it-yourself approach, where anyone who believes they can write produces copy.
2. The product specialist who knows everything there is to know about the product and usually wants to let the rest of the world know about it.
3. The communications professional who understands the market and the media, and handles some of the writing.
4. The professional writer who generally works for an outside organization and provides an independent viewpoint.

The do-it-yourself approach

DIY writers have a tendency to overuse bullet points on the basis that customers don't have time to read. Their opening shot is usually 'the copy must be short and snappy' and their favourite comment on other people's copy is that 'it doesn't flow' or 'it isn't punchy enough'. Fortunately, these arguments don't carry too much weight and there is more to effective copywriting than the punch level.

The product specialist

Product specialists can usually be found lurking in product brochures. They treat copy with tender loving care and are not usually over-concerned with punch or flow. They are, however, extremely critical of any writer who does not match up to their technical expertise.

> Information management is the set of capabilities allowing information to be modelled, stored, retrieved and interchanged. The relational database management systems are supported with provision for object-oriented databases to be supported in the future. Specifications based on ABC define the ability to manage and fully integrate all types of information: data, text, image, voice and video.

The problem is that there aren't too many customers who share the product specialist's enthusiasm for the product. Before they make a decision they need to know what it can do for their business.

The communications professional

The communications professionals play the role of go-between. They understand the market and the target audience. They understand why people buy products and services, and they know how to package information so that customers understand it easily. Here, a marketing manager is talking to customers in their own terms about the same product.

> All leading organizations today recognize the need for an information architecture. It must deliver real business benefits, support real business objectives. It must provide users with the right information, the right applications to enable them to contribute at a higher level. The architecture must be able to harness the organization's potential, its diverse skills, its accumulation of expertise. That means integrating key functions from different departments, ensuring they share aims and objectives. COMPUTALL is able to provide a single consistent interface across the many different systems in use. So it creates a common platform above which the components of the information environment are invisible.

The professional writer

The example above is halfway to helping the customer identify needs and it demonstrates a degree of understanding. But it lacks the signposts, the headlines and the customer-friendly scenarios of the earlier example (p. 18). An independent copywriter is in a unique position to transfer skills and experience from other products and markets to strengthen and simplify the copy.

PUBLICATIONS DESCRIBING PRODUCTS

Leaflets

Leaflets are a simple form of communication used in the early stages of contact with a prospect or customer. Sometimes called fliers, they summarize the key benefits of a product or service and help to create initial interest.

The leaflet can be used in response to requests for information – it ensures that prospects get introductory information, and it allows the company to follow up in more detail later. Because leaflets are so general, they can be aimed at anyone in the target audience.

Leaflets can be grouped together in a wallet – ideal when a company makes a wide range of products and wants to send targeted material to prospects. It also provides an opportunity to keep customers up to date when product information changes frequently.

Catalogues

Catalogues give customers and prospects an indication of the breadth of a product range and demonstrate that the company can deliver a complete service.

They should be seen primarily as a source of reference – the starting point for an enquiry. The catalogue should point to other publications that provide more detailed information.

Catalogues can be either helpful or extremely difficult to use. If a large weighty catalogue arrives on the customer's desk and there appears to be no simple route through it then the document will not be used to its full potential. If a company offers a vast range of similar services or products there is a good chance that the customer may not understand what he needs and end up with the wrong product. If it is clearly laid out and if it is easy to find a specific product the catalogue becomes a valuable working document for the customer.

Product brochures

Product brochures provide customers with information about products and help them to make purchasing decisions. A product brochure can give information on a single product or a range of products and it provides an opportunity to give an impression of the company as well as the product.

The product brochure is usually issued at the first or second stage in the decision-making process. It is used when customers are gathering preliminary information about products and suppliers and not yet making a detailed assessment.

The contents should cover:

- description of the product;
- how the product is used;
- main benefits to the customer;
- important achievements;

- market position;
- related products or services;
- company information;
- commercial information, such as price and availability.

Product brochures can be targeted at different members of the decision-making unit to provide each with relevant information. The chapter on target audience (p. 31) shows how to allocate the right messages to the right people.

Data sheets

Data sheets are used at a later stage in the decision-making process. They provide the detailed information that prospects need to evaluate products or make decisions.

Although data sheets have a high technical content and are often left to technical writers, they still form an important part of the communications process and should be written clearly. The most important element is the product information. Prospects compare a product or service feature by feature at this stage of the decision-making process. The information should be clearly laid out, using bullet point copy where appropriate. It should help the prospect to understand the benefits of the product and compare features with competitors' offerings.

Product guides

A product guide provides a highly detailed description of a product and can be issued to sales staff as well as customers and prospects. It can be used at the final evaluation stage of the decision-making process or issued to customers when they have bought a product.

The guide will help customers understand a product so that they can make effective use of it. For example, it can be used as a reference source for technical and design staff so that they understand characteristics, features, benefits and performance.

The product guide should include the same information as a product brochure, but the level of detail will be much higher and will include:

- description of why the product has been introduced and its main applications;
- analysis of product features;
- product operation and the skills required to use it;
- accessories, replacement parts and support services.

Technical updates

Technical updates keep the customer up to date with information on the products they have bought and ensure that the supplier communicates a policy of improvement.

Most companies treat the technical update as a routine document that needs only the minimum of editing after preparation by the technical department. However, it provides an opportunity to say 'our product has been improved and we can now offer you even greater benefit'. The information that has changed may be important to the customer, so it must be brought out clearly. If the update contains any important safety information, this should be highlighted.

The bulletin should also explain the reasons for the change – showing how the company is committed to improvement and how it works for the benefit of its customers to improve product reliability or performance.

PUBLICATIONS THAT HELP DEVELOP MARKET SHARE

Management guides

Management guides help to develop market share by helping managers to improve their skills in two areas:

1. more effective decision making;
2. managing the introduction of a new product or service effectively.

Management guides explain the management implications of a product or service showing the actions a company has to take to make the most effective use of a product or service. They show why a product has been developed and how it will contribute to solving a problem. A management guide lays down an agenda for reviewing the problem and the product; it shows who should be involved in decision making and implementation and it lists all the factors that should be taken into consideration.

Management guides play a useful role in briefing members of the prospect company who may have to use the product, but may not be directly involved in the decision-making process. Because these managers need to understand the implications of the product to make a proper contribution, they will become better prospects if they are properly informed.

Executive brochures

Executive brochures help to move the discussion of a product or service up to board level and that ensures that it receives the right attention. This helps to build relationships at the right level and is an essential element in long-term partnership.

Executive brochures review the strategic implications of new products and explain how the product will help achieve corporate goals and improve company performance. They contain little detailed product information; instead they concentrate on demonstrating the impact of the product or service on such areas as:

- new product development;
- new market opportunities;
- improved response to changes in the market;
- customer satisfaction.

These are issues that concern the board rather than the actual details of product and performance.

Sales guides

Sales guides help to improve sales performance by providing sales and distribution staff with all the information they need to understand products and sales benefits, identify prospects and decision makers and understand objections.

The sales guide should be carefully structured so that it can be used for both training and reference. It should inspire confidence in sales staff that they are selling a good product that is easy to sell and that will build the highest levels of customer satisfaction.

It should cover the following broad areas:

- market overview;
- competitive review;
- key prospects;
- buying process;
- product benefits;
- support material available.

Salesforce communications

Salesforce communications keep the salesforce up to date with developments in the company and the market-place and explain how changing conditions create new opportunities. Updates ensure that the salesforce are aware of all the factors that influence sales success by answering questions such as:

- How successful is it financially?
- How will changes in management affect the company's performance?

- What are the new products?
- What do the technical changes mean for sales potential?

The company should also take the opportunity to say to the salesforce, 'We are working hard on your behalf – these are the steps we are taking to improve your sales prospects'. The information keeps sales staff in touch with head office and ensures that they can make the most of marketing opportunities.

Dealer communications

Dealer communications help to build loyalty in the dealership. They should position a company as a business partner who wants to help the dealer develop his own business and who is genuinely interested in improving business performance. Good dealer communications will ensure that a company can achieve the highest levels of sales performance and customer satisfaction through a dealership.

Dealer communications have a number of objectives:

- communicate company policy so that dealers can operate all of the company's programmes and warranties;
- ensure that the customer gets the best possible standards of service from the dealership;
- build the right level of product information so that dealers understand product benefits and can deal with any technical queries;
- communicate sales benefits so that dealers can improve sales performance.

PUBLICATIONS DESCRIBING A COMPANY

Corporate brochures

Corporate brochures describe the company and help to convince senior executives in decision-making units that this is a successful company that is organized to manage its own business and has the skills and capability to deliver a reliable service.

A corporate brochure demonstrates corporate success so that the company can be seen as a financially stable long-term partner. Above all, it should be a statement of confidence because this is a publication that is designed to reassure customers.

A corporate brochure should include the following information:

- description of the product range that gives an indication of any successes in terms of innovation and market leadership;
- the company's locations showing its resources and international activities;

- technical and research capability;
- manufacturing resources;
- success in handling complex projects;
- financial performance;
- management skills.

SUMMARY

A company produces many different types of publication, each of which is treated with a different degree of importance. While companies would expect to take a professional approach to writing a corporate brochure or a product brochure, they leave sales guides, data sheets and salesforce communications to people without professional writing skills.

It is important to treat every publication as part of a communications programme so that it:

- builds awareness of the company's capability;
- shows the range of products available;
- makes it easy for customers to buy your products;
- ensures that sales and distribution staff are committed to selling your products.

Chapter
THREE

SETTING COMMUNICATIONS TASKS

●●●

Communications tasks help a company to achieve its marketing objectives – which in turn help it to achieve business objectives. The two should not be confused, although they are interdependent. This chapter explains how these different types of objective affect the writer's work, and provides a number of examples of communications tasks.

BUSINESS OBJECTIVES

Business objectives set the overall direction for the company, for example: to be the market leader or to set new standards in product development, or to be recognized as the leader in customer care.

This overall objective provides a framework for other people in the company – it ensures that their individual tasks are aimed at achieving the same goals. Business objectives do not stimulate action or influence people – they merely show the way forward.

Strategy

The strategy shows how the company will achieve its objectives. These might be to achieve leadership by selling at the lowest prices or by developing the best products, or by providing the highest levels of service. Individual departments can then set their own strategies within this broad framework.

MARKETING OBJECTIVES

Marketing objectives can be expressed more precisely: to increase market share by 10 per cent, or to enter a new market sector, or to develop new products for existing markets. These overall marketing objectives set the framework for more specific marketing actions. For example, to increase market share by 10 per cent might require:

- an increase in salesforce effectiveness;
- a larger distribution network;
- an incentive programme.

Increasing salesforce effectiveness might require:

- more training;
- better product information;
- stronger incentive programmes;
- greater commitment to customer service.

Relating marketing objectives to copywriting

It is important for writers to understand these objectives and to ensure that the copy reflects them. Copy alone cannot achieve an objective such as 'increase market share by 10 per cent', but it has a role to play in achieving it. The copywriter's task is determined by communications objectives.

COMMUNICATIONS OBJECTIVES

Providing more training

Communications objectives support marketing objectives. For example, one of the tasks supporting the objective of an increase in salesforce effectiveness was to provide more training. A number of actions are needed to achieve this:

- convince the executive group that an investment in sales training will result in increased turnover, profit and customer satisfaction;
- convince the sales director or manager that salesforce performance will improve through training, so it is worthwhile including training in the budget and allocating time for training;
- persuade the members of the salesforce that they will improve their own performance and opportunities through training.

This gives the writer clear guidelines on what he has to achieve.

Build commitment to customer service

It is essential that the company demonstrates high levels of customer service through the salesforce. However, the salesforce may not like the idea of building customer service because it takes them away from spending productive sales time with the customer. The communications task is to:

- convince the salesforce that an investment in customer service will improve the long-term relationship with customers and that it will ultimately improve their sales opportunities;
- communicate the fact that customer service is vital to account control.

Persuade a management team that customer care is important

The company wants to build the highest level of customer care through a network of distributors. The process begins with the dealership senior management team. The communications tasks include:

- convincing the management team that customer care will be good for dealership business;
- helping the team understand the relationship between satisfied customers and repeat purchase;
- helping the team understand that customer satisfaction is delivered by people and that the only way standards will improve is by improving the performance of the people;
- making the team aware of the importance of managing the whole process and of spreading the message throughout the whole organization.

Get staff involved in customer care

It is just as important to get the commitment and understanding of the dealership task force, because everyone in the dealership is responsible for customer care. The communications task is to:

- persuade staff that they are involved in building customer satisfaction;
- build commitment and understanding of the programme.

Communicating customer care to customers

The other important task is to convince customers that the company cares about their interests and that it is taking action to improve the levels of customer satisfaction. The communications task is to:

- convince customers that this is a caring company;
- demonstrate how customer care will provide them with the highest standards of service.

Building partnership with suppliers

A bank decides that it is going to move into the personal financial services market. It has to encourage partners to get involved to provide the right levels of expertise and professionalism. The communications task is to:

- convince them that working with the bank will provide a good business opportunity and improve their own prospects;

- encourage them to deliver the highest standards of service.

Explaining change to employees

Employees may be concerned at the impact of the changes on their own career prospects. By managing the process of change, the bank can ensure that everyone understands the reasons and the implications. The communications task is to:

- convince employees that the change will be worthwhile;
- explain that they may need to learn some new skills to deal with the new situation;
- show how the new service fits in with the rest of the bank's product range;
- demonstrate how the new service will help to establish the long term loyalty that is so important;
- describe the benefits of the new service and help staff to sell them to customers.

Introducing the new service to customers

Customers need to be told about the new service, particularly if it represents a change of direction for the bank. The communications task is to:

- make customers aware of the service;
- encourage them to make an enquiry;
- explain the benefits over other forms of personal finance and show why the product is superior.

SUMMARY

- Communications objectives provide the writer with clear guidelines on the task the copy has to achieve.
- Before dealing with communications objectives, the writer must understand business and marketing objectives.
- Every marketing task creates a range of communications objectives that vary with the target audience.

Chapter
FOUR

THE TARGET AUDIENCE

●●

Effective marketing copy ensures that the right people make the right decisions about a product or service. In business, most purchase decisions are made by groups rather than individuals, so it is important for the writer to understand the information needs of each member of the group.

This chapter will help you develop the skill of targeting copy. It will explain how to write copy that will:

- influence all the important members of a decision-making group;
- offer benefits to individual members that are relevant to their role in the company;
- talk to individual members in their own language;
- provide the group with all the information they need to make a positive decision about a product or service.

ANALYSING A TARGET AUDIENCE

Before you write any copy ask these three questions:

1. Who do I need to influence?
2. What do they need to know?
3. What action should they take?

The following section shows some of the people a writer has to influence. Each individual buyer or member of a decision making group is likely to have different concerns.

DECISION-MAKING GROUPS

A simple decision-making group might include three types of people:

1. A purchasing manager placing the initial enquiry and the final order.
2. A technical manager evaluating the product.

3. A member of the board evaluating the company as a supplier.

Contact is normally focused on the purchasing manager and the technical manager with the company relying on its corporate reputation to maintain credibility with the board.

Each of them has general concerns:

- the purchasing manager needs to know about price and delivery;
- the technical manager is interested in performance;
- the board member is interested in the capability of the company as a reliable supplier.

Purchasing managers

This is a very superficial view of the purchase decision-making process but it shows how copy can be planned to meet the information needs of people with different perspectives. To illustrate this, here is an extract from a brochure on a new distribution depot. It is aimed at purchasing managers who might be concerned about their supplier's delivery capability.

> We've just opened a brand new 3 million square feet distribution centre close to the M1/M25 interchange. The purpose-built depot will allow us to double our stockholding capacity and provide an even faster service to our clients. We're using the latest automated handling techniques to speed up order assembly. That way we can respond to requests for urgent deliveries quickly.

The copy so far includes key messages for the purchasing manager, such as:

- faster service;
- quick response to requests for urgent deliveries.

The writer then goes a stage further. The distribution depot is designed to meet the requirements of Just-In-Time or JIT, as it is known, a manufacturing technique that demands that manufacturers hold minimum stocks and the supplier provides a service on demand or at specified intervals. Research shows that many companies are unsure of the implications of techniques like JIT and need to understand how to manage the process.

> We've got the resources to handle JIT delivery. Our computerized stock control and information systems can provide up-to-date information so that we can meet scheduled and *ad hoc* deliveries integrated with your JIT schedules. We're running a series of JIT seminars at the new distribution centre and we'd like to invite you to join us.

That invitation can be invaluable if the purchasing manager is not sure about the implications of JIT. The seminar invitation adds extra value to the description of the new centre.

Technical managers

The technical manager in a simple decision-making group is also concerned about delivery and price, but these are less important compared with the quality and reliability of the product. When a manufacturing company buys a component, it usually forms part of a more complex final product. So the technical manager wants to know that each component will contribute to the best possible performance of the product.

Take a simple component, such as a valve or a bearing in a piece of machinery. If such a component fails the whole machine goes down, so the technical manager looks for reassurance about quality.

> The bearings are manufactured to meet the highest standards of performance. Each one is individually inspected and samples are destruction tested to ensure long reliable operation in normal conditions. Performance data is enclosed at the end of this brochure and special applications can be tested.

Key messages include:

- individual inspection;
- long reliable operation;
- performance data;
- special applications.

This type of information is designed to reassure the purchasing department and the technical manager. The technical manager knows that he can specify the component with confidence as part of a quality product and the purchasing department knows that they won't be reprimanded for buying an inferior product that could tarnish the company's image.

Board members

The board members in a decision-making group such as this don't get involved in details of price and performance. Their concern is that the supplier will be reliable and won't let them down at a crucial stage in the manufacturing process. Missing components can destroy a manufacturing schedule, leading to late delivery and lost customers. The board also want reassurance that the supplier is financially sound and not liable to go out of business.

> The company is the largest UK bearing manufacturer and a member of a highly successful international engineering group. The company supplies bearings to some of the most prestigious names in engineering and has an

enviable reputation for quality and innovation. We spend £1.5 million a year on research and development and have recently invested over £3 million in new manufacturing facilities. The company is a well managed, financially stable operation with a record of increasing turnover and profit for the last four years.

Changes in the decision-making structure

The above was a simple example of an industrial purchasing situation and it demonstrates the principle that copy must be written for different perspectives if it is to succeed.

However, commentators on business-to-business marketing have identified a number of trends that have made that process more complex. One of the most important is the emergence of a changing management structure in which middle managers work in project teams and undertake tasks for which they might have no professional training or previous experience. This has considerable impact on the way copy is written.

PROJECT TEAMS

The decision-making team is now far more complex. It contains the basic groups described earlier, but may also include other people who play a key role in the process. It brings together groups of senior managers, middle managers and specialist professionals.

The following is part of a brochure set that is selling a computerized manufacturing control system to a company. The sales process goes on at many different levels as the introductory team briefing brochure points out.

> As we found when we implemented the system in our own plants, JIT (an advanced manufacturing technique) is an approach to manufacturing that requires the commitment and involvement of the whole management team. JIT decisions are wide-ranging, involving the chief executive and board directors, together with managers and executives responsible for production, finance, purchasing and marketing. This brochure is for that management team, explaining the concept and benefits of JIT.

Getting the consideration of all the project team

What the writer has achieved here is to move the discussion of the product away from a narrow technical focus to management level. This will ensure that it gets full consideration by all the right people and it also positions the company as a strategically important partner rather than just a supplier of computers. The introductory brochure is deliberately designed as a discussion document rather than a sales brochure.

> JIT may require the physical reorganization of a factory as well as three important changes in management practice:

1. close co-operation with suppliers;
2. stores organized to meet line-side requirements;
3. rapid flexible response to customer orders.

Helping the project team manage the introduction of a new product

This copy is saying don't just think you simply have to buy a computer to achieve the benefits, you will have to change the way you do business. This is important because many buyers express disappointment that the product they bought has not delivered the intended business benefits. It is an important part of a manufacturer's partnership that he explains all the implications and actions needed for success. The company lists the way it can help customers achieve that effective implementation.

> *Business consultancy:* working with customers to define their business requirements and assist in the development and implementation of their business and manufacturing strategies.
>
> *Implementation consultancy:* assisting in the application of products to meet specific needs.
>
> *Training services:* providing a complete range of management and product training to assist customers to identify and exploit the strengths of their organization and its systems.

This explains in practical terms how the manufacturer can help the customer to achieve the right results. It also shows that he is not alone.

This brochure has helped to get the whole management team involved and has broadened the scope of the decision-making group. Other brochures in the series are written specifically for different members of the team and reflect their information needs and their level of understanding of the subject. In the information systems business, members of the decision-making team are categorized as computer-literate or not and the copy is written at an appropriate level.

Educating newer members of the project team

Another brochure is aimed at sales administration managers, a group who would not normally figure in the decision-making process. However, they represent one of the main users of the system and it is important to get their co-operation from the start, by showing how the product will improve their working practices.

> The competitive edge is a prime requirement for a successful business. But how relevant is it to sales order management? Isn't the department's role passive – merely to respond to pressure and demands from customers,

manufacturing and management? We believe that the sales office has a positive and crucial front line role to play in developing that competitive edge.

When that was written, the call for competitive edge was echoing around the management offices of every company in the country. The problem was that many managers thought that it had little to do with them. They either felt relieved or left out. This brochure is trying to demonstrate that they are involved and is explaining practical ways in which this can be achieved.

> First by providing a rapid and flexible response to customer enquiries and orders. As customers try to minimize their stock levels they demand short lead times, prompt delivery and the flexibility to satisfy change or unplanned orders quickly. The sales organization is the vital link between the customer and production – the right response will improve customer relations and win business in a competitive marketplace.

Relating copy to the project team's individual concerns

This is talking the language of the sales office; they understand those pressures and they are looking for a solution. But the brochure is also appealing to their sense of self-esteem. A department that is usually on the receiving end of criticism from customers and the production department is now seen as a vital element in improving customer relations.

> This is the positive role for sales management, but how can it be achieved when the pressure is on to meet daily and monthly targets? The solution lies in harnessing the right computer system to the information already existing in your organization.

The brochure describes the features and benefits of the system in relation to the sales department's day-to-day tasks. It also reassures the departmental manager that the process of change will not be harmful.

> The new system can be introduced with minimum disruption to existing working patterns; it is easy to learn and requires minimal involvement from the data processing department. Help screens provide guidance for new users who quickly become fluent with transaction codes and automated routines which speed up operations.

This reassures any departmental manager who fears chaos and disruption when computers are introduced. The result of this brochure should be a sales manager who understands how computerization will help his department and who feels that he will be able to make a more positive contribution to the success of the company. The sales manager should now support the company's product when he is involved in the decision-making process.

Making the project team aware of new services

Here is another example of a routine service that needs to go on the management agenda. It is a computer disaster survival service and the brochure is aimed at senior managers, rather than a low-level maintenance supervisor.

> It has been estimated that around one in a thousand organizations are likely to suffer a computer disaster. Their computing facilities could be unavailable for a period of time and this threatens their ability to survive. 90 per cent of all companies that have suffered a disaster and had no recovery plan subsequently went out of business. Disaster survival is a business issue because Information Technology is now closely integrated with essential business and service operations to maintain competitive edge and efficiency. Successful provision against a disaster is essential for continued profitability and possibly survival.

By incorporating industry survey results and positioning the loss of computer facilities in terms of business performance, the service becomes strategically important and one to be considered seriously at high level.

Identifying benefits for every member of a project team

When an oil company wanted to broaden the use of advanced composites – a material traditionally associated with high performance, high cost applications in the aerospace industry – they took the discussion to the whole management team and not just the designer who would be the prime target.

> Aircraft, helicopters, tennis rackets and fishing rods are among the more familiar examples of high performance products that are bringing far-reaching benefits throughout industry... Now the advanced composites technology developed for aerospace is being used to find wider application in industry, offering an attractive package of benefits to users from agriculture to medicine and from defence to marine.

This immediately makes the products more familiar and accessible to non-aerospace companies. It uses simple examples and quotes industries that are definitely not hi-tech such as agriculture. It then explains the benefits in business terms rather than technical terms.

> The composite product offers considerable improvements in weight saving, strength, stiffness and corrosion resistance over traditional materials, with the opportunity to reduce through-life costs and take dramatic steps forward in product innovation.

The emphasis is placed on improving the company's products, so helping them to be more competitive.

> Advanced composites can add value to a product, contributing to design efficiency, production engineering economies, product performance, marketing effectiveness and through-life benefits for the customer.
>
> This type of value engineering can also reduce assembly time, and so influence overall production costs. Complex structures can be fabricated without welding or riveting separate pieces together, and the versatility of composites means that future product specification and performance could be changed without costly modification to the production process.

This extract offers very clear marketing and production benefits in terms that senior executives and departmental managers can understand. The brochure is effectively setting out an agenda for discussion within the company, so that the new material is not dismissed as a designer whim.

However, the designers remain the prime target in the decision-making group and much of the brochure is written from their perspective.

> Advanced composites can improve on the performance of traditional materials in many applications, but their real potential lies in new areas where designers take an original approach to materials problems. By looking beyond production limitations and making a fundamental reassessment of the design process, designers can look to new standards of performance.

This is leading edge technology and it is a subject that is bound to get any designer excited. To build on that excitement, the brochure includes many examples of the material in action.

> Already advanced composites have proved their performance and reliability at the limits of technology, with over forty years' successful development in the aerospace industry. In their way, they're making possible advances as revolutionary as those made by iron, steel, aluminium and plastics.

This positions advanced composites as a key material in a design future and helps to establish it as an essential element in the designer's portfolio.

TARGETING THE AUDIENCE – AN OVERVIEW

This analysis of decision-making groups and project teams shows that the process of analysing a target audience is not a simple one. Here is an example of the target audience for an internal communications programme to launch a local training initiative:

- senior management;
- training and development managers;
- potential trainees.

Each member of the audience has different 'concerns', which could be business objectives, responsibilities or problems. The copy must reflect these concerns by including 'key messages' showing how the product or service provides relevant benefits. Wherever possible, the copy should ensure that the audience take specific actions – which generally means buying the product or service.

Senior management

Concerns

- Ability to deliver world-class solutions.
- Skills to meet strategic business objectives.
- Cost and time of off-site skills training.

Key messages

- Initiative is part of the company's commitment to develop world-class people and solutions.
- Broadens the scope and reach of skills training to ensure skills are available to meet business objectives.
- Cost-effective solution to specific local skills training requirements.

Intended actions

- Commit to using the service.
- Set up procedure to identify relevant skills requirements.

Training and development managers

Concerns

- Need to identify solutions to skills training requirements outside core programmes.
- Need to provide cost-effective solutions.
- Time/resource problems of off-site training.

Key messages

- Broadens the scope and reach of skills training to ensure skills available to meet business objectives.
- Complements the skills content of core programmes.

- Wide range of solutions to meet management/staff skills requirements.
- Cost-effective solution to specific local skills training requirements.

Intended actions

- Recommend the initiative as a solution to specific skills requirements.
- Help managers identify opportunities for training.
- Promote local training initiative to managers and potential users.
- Set up procedures to optimize benefits from initiative.

Potential trainees

Concerns

- Develop world-class skills to make effective personal contribution to meeting the company's business objectives.
- Optimize use of time.

Key messages

- Broadens the scope and reach of skills training to develop personal skills needed to meet business objectives.
- Wide range of solutions to meet individual skills requirements.
- Optimizes use of time by keeping training on site.

Intended actions

- Discuss training opportunities with managers/training professional.

HOW TARGETING CHANGES WITH DIFFERENT PURCHASING SITUATIONS

As well as reflecting the different perspectives of the target audience, you also need to be aware of different purchasing situations. The copy should still reflect the perspectives of different group members, but it will also take into account different stages in the marketing process.

If a company is the existing supplier, it faces a number of situations:

- maintaining normal supplier/customer relations;
- maintaining existing business against competitive threats;
- competing for new business with the same customer.

Maintaining normal supplier/customer relations

The first of these is the easiest to get wrong because the supplier can take the relationship for granted – 'Here's a copy of our latest price list!'

Here is a presentation written for an annual review meeting with an important customer.

> Over the last year we have taken a number of key actions designed to improve the service we offer you. We've completed a major technical assessment of your applications and have documented it all in this manual which is being issued to technical staff in both companies. We have also set up a new order handling system dedicated to your business... Your people dial a special number and they get through to a specialist who concentrates on your business. You asked us to consider improving our pricing structure. We have achieved this, but not by cutting prices and reducing profitability because that ultimately reduces our ability to invest in the business. Instead we have identified areas of performance improvement and cost reduction so that we can enhance the service and cut costs.

The presentation includes key messages for the three decision makers:

- Board members
  - improve the service we offer you;
  - specialist concentrating on your business;
  - performance improvements.

- Technical manager
  - major technical assessment;
  - specialist concentrating on your business;
  - performance improvements.

- Purchasing manager
  - set up new order handling system;
  - improving pricing structure.

This very positive presentation says that the supplier cares about the customer's business and is taking positive steps to add value to the relationship.

Maintaining existing business against competitive threats

If the business is under threat from competitors the company has to stress its strengths and remind the customer of the benefits of doing business. Again, it is important to look at it from the three perspectives because the competitive threat may be one dimensional – a price cut or a product improvement – and the other decision makers may prefer the original suppliers existing proposal.

> We are a long-established supplier who has built up a valuable working

relationship with all the departments in your company. We have dedicated order lines and account specialists who understand your requirements and have the experience and commitment to deal with your requests quickly. We have established technical liaison groups so that we can undertake joint technical developments and we are working with you on future plans to meet your five-year business plan.

Again, the presentation includes key messages for the three decision makers:

- Board members
  - valuable working relationship;
  - working to meet your five-year business plan.

- Technical manager
  - technical liaison groups;
  - joint technical developments.

- Purchasing manager
  - long-established supplier;
  - understand your requirements;
  - deal with your requests quickly;
  - dedicated order lines.

Since a change of supplier always involves a degree of risk, the company is saying 'Change this at your peril.' Competitors have to prove that they can offer a service that is equally wide ranging.

Competing for new business with the same customer

The third opportunity is to expand the business or meet new requirements from an existing customer. For example, technical changes in the finished product or changes to a specification could rule out the existing supplier at first sight. The onus is on the supplier to prove that they are flexible and that they can adapt to change.

> The company has a wide range of products used by many of the world's leading engineering companies. The company has a policy of continuous innovation and is deeply involved with industry groups looking at future standards and developments. While we manufacture and supply one of the widest standard ranges in the business, we also have a special projects unit which has the skills and resources to tackle new applications or one-off projects. Through continuing involvement with your technical staff and your senior management team, we have developed a deep understanding of your future business plans and your technical requirements and we are well placed to meet your changing requirements. Because we have simplified the business relationship between our two companies, we can quickly integrate the new products into our existing purchasing agreements.

This is aimed primarily at the technical manager to reassure him that the company can adapt to change, but the messages will also be important to board members and purchasing managers. The key messages include:

- involvement with industry groups;
- policy of continuous innovation;
- special project unit;
- understanding future business plans;
- well placed to meet changing requirements.

Offering new products to existing customers

If we now look at the same exercise from the company's point of view, it may be trying to break into new markets or introduce new products. The customer has to take a risk if it changes products or supplier. Here is a presentation that can build acceptance at all levels if it is selling a new product into an existing customer.

> Our new product will help you to improve your competitive advantage by introducing new levels of performance and reliability into your product. We've incorporated a revolutionary new device which has been tested in demanding military applications and is now available in commercial applications for the first time. Your equipment will be able to operate at speeds 30 per cent higher than normally available and with a guaranteed service life 25 per cent higher than anything else available on the market. The new model is currently being manufactured for stock and will be available for delivery from July. The price will be 10 per cent higher than the model you currently use but we believe this is a small price to pay for the high levels of performance and reliability you can offer your customers.

This pitch is not just saying we want to sell you a higher performance model and we're going to charge you 10 per cent more for it, it's saying that we're offering to provide you with something that will benefit your product and your business. By helping customers develop their own businesses, the company is offering a strategic advantage that is important at board level. The technical and purchasing department are reassured that the change will bring the same high standards of performance and delivery. Although the price is higher – a concern that could influence the purchasing department – it is a price increase that can be justified in terms of the increased performance it offers.

Introducing products into new markets

The arguments are similar if the company is trying to introduce new or existing products into new markets. The company has to demonstrate that its product is technically competent and offers product benefits. It also has to demonstrate its reliability as a supplier. With a new customer, the company has no record to trade on so the copywriter has to help the decision-making team. They will want an answer to the question: 'Can we do business with this company on terms that benefit our business?' The technical manager will want to know if he can specify a product like this and be sure of reliable performance, and the board will want to know that their business will not be jeopardized if there is a change of supplier.

SUMMARY

It is important that you understand who you are writing for before you begin to write copy. You should always ask three questions:

- Who do I need to influence?
- What do they need to know?
- What action should they take?

In business, most purchasing decisions are made by groups rather than individuals. A typical decision-making group consists of the following people, each looking at the product or service from a different perspective:

- purchasing managers;
- technical managers;
- board managers.

However, the group has become more complex and additional members such as finance managers, marketing managers and departmental managers are now involved. The process of influencing the purchasing decision becomes more complex and includes activities such as:

- getting the consideration of all the project team;
- helping the project team manage the introduction of a new product;
- educating newer members of the project team;
- relating copy to the project team's individual concerns;
- making the project team aware of new services;
- identifying benefits for every member of the team.

The process of targeting varies with different purchasing situations, and the concerns of the audience will change depending on whether you are:

- maintaining normal supplier/customer relations;

- maintaining existing business against competitive threats;
- competing for new business with the same customer.

Chapter FIVE

USING RESEARCH

Research can help to shape the direction and focus of copywriting. It helps writers to identify the key decision makers, their reasons for buying and their main concerns.

The following is an example of a survey carried out for a building services company into the market for their services. The company identified five different market sectors – retail, finance, government, gas/electricity and telecommunications.

Where customers buy products and services

They asked customers whether they bought centrally or locally. This was important because it indicated whether or not they would be dealing with professional buyers. If customers were buying locally the company would need to emphasize different benefits such as local service, flexibility and competitive pricing.

At a central level they would be negotiating national contracts of much higher value and they would have to stress different benefits such as quality of service, nationwide resources, track record in dealing with major customers and an ability to offer value-for-money solutions.

The answers also indicated whether they would need to use targeted direct marketing to build a series of local businesses or whether they would be making high level presentations at central level.

Importance of approvals

If research showed that most buying was handled centrally, it was quite likely that the company would have to go through stringent approval procedures to become an accredited supplier and, when it pitched for local business, it would need to position itself as an approved supplier.

Identifying decision makers

The third part of the research was concerned with identifying the main decision makers in each sector. That would enable the writer to identify the different target audiences and to get across key messages that would deal with individual buyers' key concerns.

For example, they found that in the retail market the importance of property meant that decision makers included a high proportion of surveyors, architects and other building specialists.

In the financial sector, the responsibility for building services often fell to the local branch managers who did not have professional experience in this field.

In gas, electricity and telecommunications sectors, responsibility was fairly evenly split between professionals, such as architects and surveyors, and departmental managers. It was vital then to ensure that copy was industry-focused and targeted at the right level of decision maker.

Analysing buying factors

Research showed that buying factors varied by industry and by type of decision maker. Value for money rated highly in all sectors together with price, but these were the only consistent factors.

Other factors varied by sector, so the message was clear – that messages in a general brochure would have limited value. Industry-specific publications or direct marketing would be more appropriate. Individual messages could then be built in, but each of the publications would consistently feature the message that the company offered good prices and real value for money.

Technical superiority, for example, which at first sight looked like an important factor, only ranked highly in two of the five market sectors, while quality, which had always been one of the company's main claims, appeared consistently at the bottom of every list. Any copy that led with the quality claim would be irrelevant to most readers. On the other hand, reputation and track record appeared to be important in most sectors.

Meeting customer expectations

This kind of research can be valuable in highlighting the messages that should be incorporated and ensuring that the communications meet customer expectations. It can also be disconcerting because it weakens many of the claims on which companies have traditionally built their business.

Chapter SIX

PLANNING PERCEPTIONS

Just how do you want to be seen by your customers and your staff? This question is fundamental to good copywriting because it supports all the other product and company information. For example, a local power station may be the most efficient producer of electricity in the country, but if it is polluting the environment or if it poses a long-term threat to other areas, then how is it perceived by its customers and other interested parties?

PERCEPTION VARIES BY AUDIENCE

A nuclear power station, for example, might go to great pains to explain the safety aspects of its operations – to position itself as an efficient, responsible supplier of electricity. But what have these perceptions got to do with its main product – electricity? At one level, electricity is competing with gas in certain key areas. Shouldn't electricity suppliers be concerned with the perceptions of electricity against gas? The arguments have proved to be extremely complex.

RELATING PERCEPTIONS TO RESEARCH FINDINGS

Planned perceptions must take into account more than just the basic product information. Take high street banks as an example. Their basic product is current account banking for personal customers, but all banks offer similar personal banking facilities. So the planned perception cannot be related to this basic product, as for instance:

> We are an organisation that provides current account banking for our customers.

The perception must go beyond that – it must add value to the basic product:

> We provide banking services with the personal touch.

That says much more about the service. It is important to go back to customer research. What do customers look for in the service? If personal service rated highly, it is worth using that as the planned perception. But if research showed that people preferred automated banking because it was quick and it kept them away from surly staff, then personal service would not be an appropriate perception.

BUILDING PLANNED PERCEPTIONS INTO COPY

If research shows that personal service is what customers want from their banks, how do you go about building that into copy?

Internal perceptions

The process begins inside the bank, because if staff are not able to deliver the service, then the planned perception will not work. Internal communications, recruitment and training material must all stress that the bank is committed to providing the highest standards of personal service to its customers and must show what staff have to do to achieve that. Here is an example of an introduction to a staff customer care training course.

> We depend on our people to give our customers the highest standards of customer care. Your role is crucial to the bank's future success and profitability. Each person has a unique contribution to make to the bank because our whole philosophy is based on customer service.

Customer perceptions

When the bank is in a position to offer customers a high level of service it should take every opportunity to let them know about it. For example, all bank literature should carry a strap line that emphasizes the commitment to personal service. The copy should emphasize the changes that have taken place to support the high standards of personal service.

> We're getting closer to our customers in the bank – we're taking some of our staff from behind the counter and putting them out into the office so that you can talk to people face to face about a whole range of issues. That's part of our commitment to personal service.

Here is some information on the benefits of that personal service.

> As part of our continuing commitment to personal service, we're offering a personal financial advice service. So whether you're struggling to make ends meet or wondering where to invest all that extra money, come and talk to us in confidence.

The emphasis all the time is on people because as banks move towards increasing automation their services become indistinguishable and there is no opportunity to build a competitive edge.

RELATING PERCEPTIONS TO YOUR OWN STRENGTHS

This is fine for a major organization like a bank, but how does it apply to a smaller business? Take a small engineering company that handles subcontract work for larger companies, for instance. Should it just be seen as a small low-cost supplier that only handles work for other people? That limits its growth and makes it difficult for it to compete for business with other companies. What should its planned perception be?

The company looks at its own strengths and weaknesses and decides that its main strengths are innovation and flexibility. The company has a superb record for new product development and can take on complex development tasks that competitors shy away from.

The name of the company is important. The company calls itself the Engineering Hot Shop. That is the first stage in managing its own perceptions – it is no longer a sub-contractor, but a specialist in its own right. The company brochure stresses this by showing how it has tackled special projects in conjunction with customers' engineering departments. It lists the companies it has worked for and describes the projects that reflect innovation.

REFLECTING CUSTOMERS' NEEDS

The training department of a major airline wanted to work more closely with travel agents. It found through research that its courses were not seen as relevant to the needs of travel agents and it knew from booking levels that there was room for improvement.

The company undertook a programme of research and used the findings to build partnership through a customized training support service. Its planned perception was that of a training partner who worked with travel agents to develop their own business.

CHANGING ESTABLISHED PERCEPTIONS

Sometimes a company has an established reputation in one sector but needs to change this when it wants to move into new markets with the same customers. When customers have dealt with the same company for years they perceive that they provide a certain type of service and that their capability may be limited to that service.

When a computer services company wanted to expand its traditional maintenance role into a broader range of consultancy and project management services it had to compete with different types of company. For example, it wanted to offer information systems consultancy because that ensured involvement in the target company's business plans and provided contact at senior management level. This type of work was traditionally handled by management consultants who had a reputation for strategic work.

Reflect market requirements

They looked at the requirements for successful consultancy: independence, practical understanding of information systems issues, an ability to work at strategic level, industry experience and the capability to implement complete solutions. If they were to succeed in that market that was how they had to be seen. The communications focused on this.

> We are organized by vertical market so that we gain a deep understanding of our customer's business markets. Our consultants have come from industry backgrounds and have all worked at senior management level, but they also have the practical understanding of information systems issues. Here is a brief profile of the projects they have worked on ... That means our consultants are qualified to give impartial advice on the business implications of your information system.

Add differentiators

The above copy helps the company to be perceived as being as professional and impartial as a management consultancy. However, to take themselves beyond the management consultancy they need to add another dimension to the planned perception. They decide that the vital edge is their practical experience in information systems. Their consultants have the full research and technical experience of an information systems company to draw on and they have a full understanding of all the practical implications of an information systems installation.

> Our consultants have the understanding and the technical capability to enable you to get the most out of your systems - you have access through the consultants to some of the leading specialists in information systems.

Make your product or service important to customers

The company is now perceived as a strategic consultant with considerable skills in information systems. They also offer other services such as managed service, project management and applications development. The problem is that the customer may not realize that these services are important and may not consider them appropriate to his needs. This time the company has to develop a planned perception of the service and not of the company.

> Services can help you better achieve your business objectives. They ensure that all the services are there to help you meet all the requirements of installation. Because we deliver the service, you can make better use of your own resources and this can be more effective.

The company explains that it is better if a specialist organization delivers the service and stresses that the proper use of services will help a company make the most of its investment in information systems. This argument positions information systems services as a topic that should be discussed at board level.

Demonstrate capability in the new field

When the company has proved that what it is offering is important, then it has to prove its own capabilities. The planned perception then is that of a flexible service company with the skills and resources to deliver the highest standards of service.

> We are the leading European information systems services company and we have an enviable track record in delivering a complete range of quality services. We have made a major investment in service infrastructure, technology and training so that we can provide the highest levels of service everywhere.

Get the commitment of your staff

It isn't just customers who need to know about the new service – it is important that employees are aware of the changes and their role in them.

> The company is committed to providing a new range of services. We need to do this to build up a partnership with customers so that we can maintain our business at an even higher level of growth and profitability. To achieve that, we need to become a full services company and that will require considerable training to acquire the new skills. We also need to improve our service performance and we will be introducing new standards and new quality systems so that we achieve the highest levels of customer satisfaction. This initiative will ensure that you can enjoy greater involvement in the future of the company and develop your own personal skills.

These activities are carefully planned to change the perception of the company from a maintenance organization to a full service company that offers strategically important services.

EXAMPLES OF PLANNED PERCEPTIONS

Pasta

Pasta is an Italian food which was known primarily to spaghetti eaters. When marathon runners started to use it as a convenient source of carbohydrates before a race, perceptions about it changed. The copywriter's role is to establish pasta as an alternative to staple foods such as potatoes and to build this perception among people who want a healthy lifestyle.

The planned perception is 'Pasta will provide me with higher energy levels, I should eat it instead of potatoes. I will use it with other healthy foods such as salads and lean meat as part of a healthy diet.'

Business airline

An airline company established that much of its traffic came from business travellers. However, it was offering a service to both business and private passengers and this meant that the airline did not present a clear identity to either group and its investment was split between the two. The airline decided that it would be more profitable to concentrate on building up just one aspect of its business so it focused on business travel.

The positioning task was to convince business travellers and travel agents that the airline now specialized in business travel. All the actions and support tasks were geared towards supporting the business traveller. For example, destinations were concentrated on key business centres with conveniently timed flights. Arrival and departure times were planned to coincide with business hours and, for the greater convenience of passengers, a local transport infrastructure was designed to get people to and from the main business centres.

Advertisements, press relations, direct mail and other marketing communications supported the proposition that this was the business traveller's airline.

Builders' merchants

Builders' merchants were seen as forbidding places where only qualified tradesmen could venture because they understood the language and the products. They were perceived by the public as places where only heavy building products were sold. When DIY superstores opened for business they posed a serious threat, because they attracted not only consumers, but also trade customers who wanted other 'consumer' products.

The builders' merchants had to reposition themselves to the trade and to consumers. They had to prove to the trade that they could offer a superior service by stocking all the products needed to do a job. They also had to demonstrate that they provided a high standard of service and that they could supply better quality 'consumer' products, which builders could buy on their customers' behalf.

Consumers wanted a more open atmosphere – a retail environment where they could look at products and services themselves. Consumers also wanted helpful advice on selecting the right product for the job, as well as facilities such as home delivery of heavy products at convenient times.

The overall aim of the builders' merchants was to reposition themselves as professional DIY centres meeting the requirements of the trade and consumers.

Bank mortgages

Building societies were seen as the traditional suppliers of home mortgages. People saved with building societies, then took out their mortgage. Banks saw this as a lucrative market because it would broaden their customer base, increase customer loyalty and provide an opportunity to sell related services such as insurance and mortgage protection.

Banks had to reposition themselves because customers believed they only dealt with current accounts, overdrafts and personal loans. Communications had to say that they were really keen on helping people get a mortgage – they had the expertise to give independent advice on the right sort of mortgage and they also had the back-up services to provide a complete 'homeowner' service.

To give themselves a competitive edge, they had to position themselves as a faster and more flexible alternative to building society lending. In that way, they would be able to convert not only traditional bank customers, but also people who were dealing with other lenders.

Sports and leisure business

When a company well known for its sportswear decided to move into leisure clothing, it needed to show both the trade and consumer that it was a serious contender. The leisure clothing was designed to strengthen the company's brand image and attract incremental revenue from the same customer groups.

The trade had to be convinced that the company was offering a good range and that the quality of the products would reflect well on their business and the sportswear brand. They also needed to be convinced that the two product lines complemented each other and that there was a mutual compatibility. Consumers should perceive that the company's leisurewear makes the grade as fashion and that it is the same quality as the sportswear.

Petrol company

A petrol company decided that its future was not just in selling petrol but in providing motorists with a complete travel service. This included not only petrol, but also motoring related products, food, drink, maps and other products that people on the move need.

This positioned them as a convenience store and it also helped them to attract a broader audience. This is part of a long-term positioning of garages and service stations as small local businesses.

SUMMARY

By planning perceptions, you can influence the way in which your customers and your staff view your company and its products and services. Research can be used to identify current perceptions and you can then plan a programme that will move your audience towards the planned perception. However, it takes more than just planning; the positioning messages must be built into every form of communication and every publication should be reviewed for consistency.

The key stages in building a planned perception are:

- identifying the way in which perception varies by audience;
- relating perceptions to research perceptions;
- building planned perceptions into copy;
- relating perceptions to your own strengths;
- reflecting customers' needs;
- changing established perceptions by
  - reflecting market requirements;
  - adding differentiators;
  - making your product or service important to customers;
  - demonstrating capability in the new field;
  - getting the commitment of your staff.

Chapter SEVEN

AUDITING COPY

A communications audit is used to check whether copy is achieving its communications objectives and building planned perceptions.

The following is an example of an internal communications audit that will act as the basis for planning or modifying the copy that supports customer relations programmes.

BACKGROUND

Effective customer relations are important to long-term success and profitability. One of the most important elements in customer relations is the attitude and commitment of staff who are in direct or indirect contact with customers. Their performance and attitudes have a direct impact on the customer's overall perception of a company. Poor standards of service, lack of product or company knowledge when dealing with customer queries, or bad handling of customer complaints can destroy any gains made through effective external communications.

The following is a recommendation for an internal communications audit that would be used to identify the potential for improving customer relations through an effective internal communications programme.

The programme will be aimed primarily at staff who are in contact with customers. It will focus on communications needed to develop positive attitudes towards customer relations and ensure understanding of:

- changes in company strategy;
- new products;
- changes in operations.

SCOPE OF THE AUDIT

The audit will seek to establish a framework for an internal communications programme. It should cover these topics:

- Who influences customer perceptions and attitudes?

- What attitudes should those key staff hold?
- What is the target customer perception of your staff?
- What product/market/business knowledge do those staff need?
- What are the most effective channels for communicating that information?

To demonstrate how the audit operates, here are examples of how three of those topics could be handled:

1. What is the level of awareness of key messages?
2. How consistently are key messages presented in existing internal communications?
3. How effectively do the communications support the customer relations process?

AUDITING INTERNAL AWARENESS OF KEY ISSUES

It is important that key messages relating to corporate strategy, product range and operating procedures are understood and presented consistently throughout the company. Research should be carried out to assess the understanding of these issues at various levels, particularly in departments responsible for customer contact.

Objectives

- Identify key internal audiences.
- Assess level and effectiveness of current communications.

Issues

How well do key people understand:

- the company's strategy;
- product range;
- operating procedures?

Technique

Hold interviews with selected people from:

- marketing and communications staff;
- staff responsible for customer contact.

Response

If the audit shows that understanding of the issues is low amongst the target audience, the communications programme must be reassessed. Copy must concentrate on building understanding of those issues.

AUDITING CONSISTENT PRESENTATION OF KEY MESSAGES

The audit looks at the content of current internal communications projects to ensure that they reflect the key messages and are relevant to the information needs of the target audience.

Objectives

- Measure how consistently key messages are communicated.
- Identify mechanisms for controlling communications consistency.

Issues

How consistently are the messages presented in the following media:

- staff newspapers;
- database information;
- branch communications;
- other employee communications;
- product training material;
- team briefing material?

Technique

- Review published material.
- Interview communications managers/authors.

Response

If the audit shows that messages are not presented consistently, the content of each piece of communication should be carefully reviewed against a checklist of key positioning messages. Future versions of those communications should be rewritten for consistency.

AUDITING EFFECTIVE SUPPORT OF CUSTOMER RELATIONS

Considerable opportunities exist for developing effective customer relations through key staff. The audit should assess the level of awareness of customer relations and look at the potential for increasing motivation to build customer satisfaction. The audit should consider whether the information key staff receive is relevant to their information needs, and whether it is presented in a convenient, persuasive form. The audit should consider all the channels of internal communication available to assess which would be the most effective for key messages.

Objective

- Measure the contribution of current internal communications to effective customer relations.

Issues

- Do staff understand customer relations issues?
- Are they aware of existing support material?
- Do they find support material useful?
- What are their information requirements?

Technique

- Interviews with key staff and managers.
- Audit of use of support material.

Response

If the audit shows that staff are not making effective use of the customer relations support material, communications should concentrate on explaining the material available and the way it can be used to improve customer relations.

SUMMARY

A communications audit gives a valuable opportunity to measure the effectiveness of current internal communications. Although the audit looks at the current situation in a company, it should be seen as part of a continuing process to ensure that internal communications are effective and provide value for money. The audit can lay down a clear framework for internal communications, defining required perceptions, target audiences, communications tasks and priorities. The internal communications plan and its implementation should be measured against that framework.

Chapter
EIGHT

LANGUAGE

••

Language in copywriting has to find a careful balance between personal preference and corporate style. There is rarely a 'right' word or phrase to describe a product or service. However, there is a 'language framework' that can be applied to products and services. This framework covers the content, tone and key messages that ensure effective communication.

This section examines the language framework for three important topics:

1. Quality.

2. Customer care.

3. The impact of technology.

You can use the advice given here to write copy for specific marketing situations.

THE LANGUAGE OF QUALITY

Quality has been a key issue for many years but it is still in its infancy in communications terms. Many companies claim to be quality led but few are getting the real communications benefits from that. Quality should be seen as a benefit to the customer, not to the supplier – it helps to reassure customers that they will get a consistency of service or product that is measured against independent external standards.

Demonstrate conformance to independent standards

Conformance to a recognized quality standard can be valuable in competitive situations and makes it easier to get approval when several suppliers are competing for the same business. In some markets quality registration may be a condition for doing business. Quality registered firms have already demonstrated that they can work to certain quality standards and this gives them an immediate advantage over their competitors.

> We are approved to independent quality standards throughout the company.
> That means you can be certain of getting the highest standards of service

from every department you deal with and it's your independent guarantee that the service will be right.

Show the scale of your commitment to quality

> As an organization, we're committed to quality and every one of our employees has been through an intensive quality training programme that took thousands of man hours. That is a mammoth effort but it means we can be confident of giving you the highest standards of service.

This company is demonstrating its practical commitment by showing the extent of its training programmes and is also showing that it understands quality is a customer benefit.

Explain quality in specific terms

> We're a quality legal practice; we've registered all our most important processes to independent standards so that you get the right response. For example, we're obliged to reply to any of your requests within three days and services such as searches, documentation and other actions must be completed within a specified time-frame. We like to think that gives you a better standard of service and ensures that you get the legal service you need to run your own business efficiently.

Once again this is pitching quality in terms of customer benefits and ensuring that customers really understand the practical implications of quality.

Demonstrate that quality is consistent throughout a company

Quality should be focused on people so that customers know they will get a good response whenever they contact the company.

> We pay a great deal of attention to people care and training so that the people you deal with are all quality people. We're committed to raising the standards of all our departments and we're undertaking a comprehensive training programme so that every time you deal with us you're dealing with quality people. By investing in the best people and matching that with the highest levels of support, you'll get the best from the partnership.

The key word here is confidence because customers know they are dealing with a defined quality that will provide the highest standards.

THE LANGUAGE OF CUSTOMER CARE

Customer care is one of the major driving forces in business today. Companies want to retain the loyalty of their customers to ensure repeat purchases and long-term business growth and they do it through a policy of customer care. At its simplest level, it is an expression of an attitude, showing that you care about your customers, make them feel welcome, thank them for shopping with you, and show that you are grateful for their custom. However, these are superficial and it is important to offer customers benefits that are more tangible.

Offer the customer convenience

Real customer care involves making customers feel they have got something over and above the product when they shop with you. Here is a message from a store:

> We aim to make shopping more convenient for our customers – we've got longer opening hours, increased parking, much more variety in store and you'll find a restaurant and a bank where you can take care of your other needs while you're shopping.

In short, the store is doing a lot of things to make shopping more convenient for the customer. When customers compare stores they won't just compare prices or the quality of food, they will consider the whole shopping experience.

Go beyond the basic service

Take, for example, a garage where they offer you a courtesy car when your car is in for service or repair.

> We know from talking to our customers that inconvenience is the biggest single problem in servicing – you haven't got a car so you're not mobile and you depend on public transport or other people. If you drive on business, you may have to reorganize your schedule to suit the servicing of your car. But when you book a service with us, inconvenience is a thing of the past. We'll provide you with a loan car for as long as your car is in the workshop – free of charge – all you pay for is the petrol and insurance. So put an end to the hassle and get the courtesy service from us.

This copy recognizes a problem that research has identified and shows that the garage is prepared to do more than just service your car. In that way the garage is differentiating itself from other garages that only provide the basic service. It is recognizing customers' real needs and demonstrating that it can meet them.

Explain the benefits of co-operation

In business, customer care is sometimes taken to the level of partnership and here the company shows that working together can be to the mutual benefit of both parties.

> We want to work in long-term partnership with you so that we can understand your changing business requirements and develop our services

to meet your real needs. Your business goes through a life cycle and we are able to help you at every stage of that life cycle.

Offer specific benefits

It is important to express customer care in specific terms.

> By working with our specialists, your staff can improve their own skills. Also we can carry out the tasks that are not strategically important, leaving your staff free to run your core business activities. That makes for a cost-effective solution and makes better use of your own scarce resources.

This explains the potential benefits of working in partnership in specific terms, by showing customers how they can overcome a recognizable problem.

Provide reassurance for your customers

Companies can make it easier for their customers to deal with them by simplifying the process of buying and getting information.

> We've introduced a new telephone system so that you now have to make only one contact to reach anyone in the organization. You don't have to remember separate numbers or work out who you need to contact, just tell us what your query is and we'll put you in touch with the right people. If someone isn't actually available to deal with your query straight away. we'll arrange for the appropriate people to get back to you within a specified time. So whatever your query – if you've got a service fault, want to order something or make a general enquiry – just dial this one number wherever you are in the UK and your call will be handled at local rates.

There are a lot of comfort factors in this copy – the customer doesn't have to know a name or a number – nor will he get passed from one department to another or left hanging on the end of an empty line that keeps on ringing. These are all common occurences and by recognizing them and offering a solution the company is demonstrating customer care.

Make your products easy to use

When customers are faced with a new and potentially complicated product, you can demonstrate customer care by helping them make use of it.

> You'll find all our new power tools come complete with an illustrated instruction manual that you can use to work on your own project. The tool also has built-in features that make it easy for you to get accurate results first time – speed controls, depth gauge, and self-cleaning devices so that your work is more accurate. When you buy one of our power tools we want you to enjoy the best results in the quickest possible time.

The features on these power tools are probably no different to those available on any other power tool, it's just that the company is positioning them as customer care benefits.

Ask for the customer's opinion

By inviting comments on your products or services, you show that you care about your customers' views.

> We aim to deliver the highest levels of customer satisfaction. If anything about our product or service lets you down, please let us know – we like to have your opinions so that we can continually improve our service and provide you with the finest products available.

Involve your customers in the development of your business

As well as asking for your customers' opinions, you can also demonstrate that you respond to comments.

> We have a policy of product development which concentrates on customers. At the beginning of each quarter, we will let you know about our current development plans. If you want to provide any comments then we can build these into our planning process – that way we can integrate our planning process with your product development programme so that we can continue to meet your business requirements.

THE LANGUAGE OF BUSINESS TECHNOLOGY

Do business people buy technology or do they buy benefits? It can be difficult for companies to describe products that they have spent years developing in their research labs as anything less than a major technical breakthrough, but technology is irrelevant unless it solves someone else's problems.

The arrival of the world's most powerful computer is great news for anyone interested in computing for its own sake, but how many businesses can afford to collect expensive toys? However, if you announce this new computer as the quickest way to process a payroll accurately with minimal staff involvement, then that is a significant business benefit.

Relate benefits to the target audience

New materials may be startling in their properties and fascinating to scientists and metallurgists, but what will they do for a chief executive? A material that is stronger and lighter than anything else on the market will have obvious benefits in the aerospace industry, but it can also be used to develop new lightweight applications in traditional engineering. That could give chief executives an opportunity to speed up their product development programme and enter new markets with very competitive products.

Marketing managers get excited when they see business benefits in new technology. A new metal that is so strong and durable that it is virtually maintenance free allows the marketing manager to offer his customers improved levels of reliability and that reflects well on customer satisfaction.

If you can say of your product that, 'This is a low-maintenance product that costs more at the outset but is cheaper when whole life costs are analysed', then this is an argument that is likely to appeal to a finance director and a technical director – the benefits of the same material are being passed down the line to the people involved in the purchasing process.

Show how technology can re-shape a business

When computers were first offered to banks, one of the major attractions was not that they automated tasks, but that they gave them the opportunity to change the whole direction of their business.

> By automating many of the more routine activities like accounts, processing, cash withdrawals, the computer can free key staff for front office activities. This is in line with your strategy of building better customer relations by offering a more personal service.

The banks are being offered technology not for its own sake but as a means of providing customers with a better service.

Using technology to offer a personal service

Service stations are beginning to realize that they can deliver a higher standard of personal service to customers by using computers at the point of sale.

> By installing a customer information service at the point of sale you can give your customers a better standard of service. By retaining customer files you can respond to a service request quickly. 'Mr Clark, your car is due for its 36,000-mile service. Last time we replaced the shock absorbers, so we'll check the tyres as well for you. And that new radio we fitted for you, are you enjoying it? By the way, for models like yours, we're doing a special offer on accessories. I'll send you the catalogue before you come in next week and if anything needs fitting we'll do that free of charge ... Morning, Mr Smith, you've got a problem with the door lock. Right, we can sort that out immediately – we had a service bulletin last week and it only needs a small adjustment – we'll take care of it free of charge. You won't have to make an appointment but if you'd like to give us a ring before you come in we'll make sure you're not kept waiting.

This is using technology to deliver real business benefits of improved customer service. Information on the customer, the car, promotional offers, service records and any alerts are available on screen.

Balancing technology with personal service

An interesting use of technology came when mainframe computer manufacturers introduced remote diagnostics on their computers.

> By monitoring the condition of your computer automatically, we can identify when faults are likely to occur and if something does go wrong, we can send an engineer with a complete diagnosis and all the spare parts needed. Certain faults can be corrected remotely without a visit.

To the customer, this is a real benefit – the equipment will continue to operate reliably and any problems will be resolved quickly and efficiently. But there is a downside to this. Customers are used to personal service – the sight of an engineer on site is reassuring – it assures the customer that they are getting the right level of service. But when something happens remotely, the level of service doesn't always get noticed. Customers may think that they are paying for something that doesn't exist.

SUMMARY

A 'language framework' provides a basis for checking copy. It helps to ensure that the copy is communicating effectively with the target audience. The language framework uses tried and tested approaches to writing that can be applied to any product or service.

Chapter NINE

DEVELOPING KEY MESSAGES

Key messages are a foundation of good copywriting; they ensure that the reader gets the information that is essential for decision making. The key messages can be the most important benefits of the product or they might be positioning messages that help to build a planned perception of the company.

To determine the key messages, look at the product from the reader's perspective. Determine the most important benefits of the product and why they would persuade the person to buy that product. These vary from product to product and also vary according to perspective. So the same product can have a number of different key benefits, depending on the readership.

This section looks at the process of developing key messages for a number of different product groups.

EXAMPLE 1: LAWN-MOWERS

Lawn-mowers have a domestic market, a professional market and a local authority market. Each type of buyer looks for different benefits.

Domestic users

In the domestic market, the real battle is between different forms of powered mowers – cylindrical and rotary. Their key messages have evolved with product development and with the changes in competitive activity.

For example, a key message for cylindrical mowers was convenience. Early hover mowers didn't have a grass collector so the gardener had to clear up the cuttings afterwards – hence the well-known phrase 'less bovver than a hover'. The hover mowers could retaliate with lightweight, speedy operation. That was their key message.

However, gardeners are concerned with the finish and the convenience. When hover mowers added the convenience of grass collection the focus shifted to the quality of finish. Rotary mowers promised a striped finish, hovers, their competitors claimed, just cut the grass. But when hover technology was able to provide the striped finish as well, the differences became more marginal.

This is a selection of key messages suitable for that market:

- The mower provides a superb striped finish.
- The mower is more convenient because it collects the cuttings.
- This lightweight mower is ideal for elderly people.
- This mower is quick and easy to use – it's like using a vacuum cleaner on your lawn.

The professional market

The professional market includes groundsmen, professional gardeners and others who use a mower to earn their living. They are unlikely to be concerned with speed and convenience because they are judged ultimately on the quality of their work. People who prepare tennis courts or golf courses need to achieve specific results – they are concerned with quality of finish and control over the finished surface.

The key messages for this market include:

- Specially designed for the professional groundsman.
- Carefully balanced blades for the finest surface finish.
- Enables you to achieve carefully-controlled results.

The local authority market

When councils buy mowers they are likely to use them to maintain large areas of grass. They will be less concerned with quality of finish, although they may have sports areas to maintain. They look closely at overall operating costs and reliability. Reliability means less downtime and faster grass cutting which, in turn, cuts down labour costs.

Key messages for this sector might include:

- Low cost of ownership.
- Spare parts are readily available.
- These mowers are built to last.
- The mowers have a three-year extended warranty.
- They use the finest components for complete reliability.
- The mowers are simple to maintain.

EXAMPLE 2: COMPUTERS

Computers have three distinct areas of use – home computing, professional and business. In the business sector there are further sub-divisions by job function.

Home computing

The home computer market grew rapidly during the 1980s. At the outset, it was important to stress the generic benefits of home computing – the opportunity to play games, use educational software or put domestic information such as household accounts on a permanent record. These key messages ensured that people understood that buying a computer was an important purchase.

As the home market matured, the key messages were built around the performance of the machine and the software that was available for it. A computer with 6000 colours and a high resolution monitor was important for someone who wanted the advantages of high-speed computer games. Hundreds of titles available was important because rival home computers were incompatible with each other. A new model had to have lots of supporting software otherwise it was of limited value.

Key messages for the domestic market include:

- Ideal for the childrens' education.
- Superb games capability.
- Extensive collection of software available.
- Easy to use.
- Hours of entertainment.

Computer professional

Messages about performance are even more important to the professional computer user. The computer professional understands the technology of computing and makes use of advanced features.

Key messages for this sector include:

- Operating speed is ...
- The powerful memory takes care of the most demanding applications.
- It is compatible with most major systems.

Business users

As with any purchasing decision, business users assess computers from a number of different perspectives including those of: senior executives, departmental managers, users and service staff.

Senior executives

Senior executives are concerned with what the computer can do for the organization's competitive edge. How can it improve the company's business performance? Buying a computer system is a major investment so they are looking for a means of justifying that investment.

Key messages for them include:

- The computer system can be integrated with your existing installation.

- The system will help to improve your response to changing business conditions.

- The system will help you manage your business more effectively.

Departmental managers

The departmental manager needs to know how the computer will affect his department's efficiency and how much support he will have to enjoy a smooth introduction.

Key messages for them include:

- The system will improve the efficiency of your department.

- Your staff will be more productive.

- Staff will quickly adapt to the new system.

- The system can be easily integrated with your existing working practices.

Users

Users want to know that the computer is both powerful enough to meet all their requirements, and easy to use. Users want to know that it will enhance their professional performance and help them do their job better. They are not concerned with technical specifications – they only want the benefits.

Key messages for the computer user include:

- Allows you to run most popular business programmes.

- Improves your decision making.

- Simple to learn but capable of advanced performance.

Service staff

The service manager needs to know that the computers are reliable and easy to maintain; ideally they will be compatible with other equipment already installed and they should not require new skills to support them.

Key messages for service staff include:

- The system can be easily integrated with existing systems.

- Full service support is available for the product.

- The system incorporates features to ensure reliable operation.
- The system can be maintained by semi-skilled staff.

EXAMPLE 3: FURNITURE

Domestic furniture, office furniture and architect/designer furniture all require different approaches.

Domestic furniture

Domestic furniture enhances the home and reflects people's life-styles. People choose kitchen furniture, for example, for many different reasons – it may be well constructed so that it lasts a lifetime, it could be well designed so that it provides optimum storage capacity, it could be aesthetically pleasing so that it blends in with certain types of decor, or it could represent real value for money – giving the owner a complete kitchen for a ridiculous price.

Key messages for this market might include:

- This furniture will enhance your home.
- Superb continental styling to add that touch of luxury.
- Functional furniture that looks good.
- Value-for-money furniture that gives you a complete room for just...
- Styling that enhances any decor.

Office furniture

Office furniture is bought for more rational reasons. It should be highly functional, providing an efficient working environment that helps to build productivity at work. It might be ergonomically designed to meet current legislation on health and safety at work, or it could be stylish but functional so it creates an attractive working environment and shows a caring attitude. System furniture is positioned as cost effective because it can be reorganized or supplemented as the company grows. This is valuable when an organization is likely to change every couple of years or less.

Key messages for the office furniture market include:

- Flexible systems to meet changing business needs.
- Attractive styling to enhance the working environment.
- Robust construction to provide long life.
- Modular system to grow with your business.
- Ergonomically designed to boost productivity.

Designer furniture

Designer furniture is aimed at architects and interior designers who specify furniture for other people. Generally price is less important in this market because designers are only brought in to work on more important projects. Style and functionality are more important because the designer is being judged on his sense of style and his ability to meet a specific brief.

Key messages for designers and architects include:

- Appeals to discerning buyers.
- Winner of international design awards.
- Suitable for a variety of prestige projects.
- Individual styling.

EXAMPLE 4: ACCOUNTANCY SERVICES

Accountancy services are used by self-employed people, small businesses and large corporations.

Self-employed people

Self-employed people may see accountants as an expensive luxury. It is important to stress that a professional service is essential and that this can take away much of the paperwork headaches that affect individuals. The accountancy firm must not appear so large that it overwhelms the individual but it should have the experience to provide a service over and above what the individual could do himself.

Key messages for the self-employed include:

- An efficient way of managing finances.
- Specialist service that is essential for busy self-employed people.
- Service specially developed for self-employed people.

Small business services

Small businesses have more wide ranging needs so it is important that they are offered more than just an accounting service. They should be able to find advice on cash flow, borrowing, funding the business, and preparing forecasts and business plans. In other words, the accountant should be seen as an adviser.

Key messages for small businesses include:

- A full range of accountancy services.
- Comprehensive advice and guidance on small business finance.

- Support with financial management.
- Extensive experience in the small-business sector.

Accountancy services for major clients

When the customer is a large corporation, business support is even more important. Large accountancy practices have become more like management consultancies, offering their clients a broad range of financial and advisory services.

Key messages for large corporations include:

- A broad range of financial and management services.
- Partners with wide-ranging business experience.
- Services to meet changing business requirements.
- A network of international offices to provide global service.

EXAMPLE 5: BUSINESS CREDIT CARDS

Business credit cards can help a company control its cash flow and manage its business expenditure. The card programme should have a flexible structure so that different cards can be given to staff at different levels in the company. Companies have different reporting and management requirements so a card system must accommodate a broad spectrum of needs. There are three distinct groups of users – companies who are new to credit cards, companies with large numbers of users and companies with a strong hierarchical structure.

Companies who are new to cards

There may be an initial task in selling the generic benefits to companies who have not used credit cards before. The copy would have to explain the benefits of credit cards over cash, advances, accounts and other forms of payment.

Key messages for new users include:

- Credit cards give you greater control over business finance.
- Credit cards are an integral part of a financial control system.
- Credit cards are more secure and flexible than cash.

Companies with large numbers of users

With larger customers, the messages can be varied according to the way the company is organized. For example, a company with a large number of sales regions would find it convenient to have a credit card programme that incorporated large amounts of management information. They could then have an easy way of analysing their expenditure by region, by individual, and by type of expenditure. This can provide the basis for controlling their expenditure more closely and also for negotiating deals over frequent purchases such as hotel accommodation or petrol.

Key messages for this group include:

- Credit card systems provide high levels of management information.
- Management information can help you to control operating expenditure more efficiently.
- Credit card programmes enable you to identify areas that require greater management attention.

Companies with a hierarchical structure

Flexible credit card systems with different levels of card are ideal for companies with a complicated staff structure. If, for example, the company had a large number of people operating in export markets they would be able to utilize the international payments system to manage their overseas travel and entertainment expenditure and save money on unnecessary currency dealings. Senior staff could be given gold cards that included special privileges, while sales staff or delivery drivers could be given cards with expenditure limited to specific items such as travel and accommodation. The benefit to the customer is that the credit card programme can be customized to the needs of individual companies.

Key messages for this sector include:

- Card systems can be tailored to the needs of individual customers.
- Payment and financial control systems can be built around credit cards.
- Customers can meet the credit card requirements of all their staff.

EXAMPLE 6: TRAINING SERVICES

Training services are bought by companies at a number of different levels. The people who are involved in the decision include senior executives, departmental managers and the trainees themselves.

Senior executives

Senior executives need to know that the training will improve the company's competitive edge, by ensuring that staff have the skills and knowledge to meet business objectives. Training must be shown as a strategic activity that is an investment in future success.

Key messages for senior executives include:

- Training is a strategic activity designed to build the competitive edge.
- Training is an integral part of a people care policy.
- Training provides the skills to meet future business objectives.

Departmental managers

Departmental managers need to know that their departments will be better equipped to achieve their specific targets. Departments are under pressure to handle increasing workloads with limited resources.

Key messages for departmental managers include:

- Training can help you make the most of limited resources.
- Training can help you develop scarce skills.
- Training will help you to meet your departmental objectives more effectively.

Trainees

Trainees need to know that they will improve their personal skills and performance by training. This will provide opportunities for personal development and ensure that they can make a more effective contribution to the company.

Key messages for trainees include:

- Training will improve your personal skills.
- Through training you will be able to make a more effective contribution to the company.
- Training will provide you with enhanced career opportunities.

EXAMPLE 7: VIDEO CAMERAS

Video cameras are used by professionals and businesses as well as domestic users. The type of equipment is the same, but the specification varies and the applications are different.

Domestic users

Domestic users need to be reassured that they will be able to use the equipment easily without making complete fools of themselves. They also want to know that they can achieve good results without taking a course in film direction. Early home video messages concentrated on the benefits of this new form of technology that allowed people to capture moving images easily and replay them without waiting. That stage has passed and the emphasis now is on the growing simplicity and sophistication of video cameras.

Key messages for domestic users include:

- Video cameras allow you to keep those treasured memories for ever.
- Video cameras are simple to use.
- Video cameras have a host of automatic features that enable you to achieve superb results whatever the conditions.

Professional users

The professional wants equipment that is reliable, robust and sophisticated enough to produce the best possible results time after time.

Key messages for professionals include:

- This camera features the latest digital technology to produce the best possible results.
- The camera is built for long reliable operation in all conditions.
- The camera is part of a complete system of integrated components that enable you to build the video kit you need.

Business users

Business users need initial guidance on how video can benefit their business – to improve the quality of training or presentation for example. When they select equipment, they are looking for reliable cameras that are simple to use, but produce quality results.

Key messages for business users include:

- Video will improve the quality of business presentations and training.
- The video camera is designed to produce high quality results, but is simple to operate.
- The camera is extremely reliable and is guaranteed for long-life operation.

EXAMPLE 8: LEISURE CENTRES

Leisure centres attract customers from schools and the general public.

Schools

Schools are looking for low-cost facilities where pupils can try out a variety of sports. The ideal leisure centre offers not only good facilities, but also coaching expertise so that pupils will be in safe hands and will learn the right skills. The centre should be in a convenient position and should offer special opening hours so that schools can integrate this into their own activities.

Key messages for schools include:

- The leisure centre offers a complete range of sports.
- The centre is well-equipped and has a staff of fully qualified coaches.
- Coaching courses can be integrated with school physical education programmes.

General public

The public will be attracted by a wide choice of activities and the opportunity to progress from basic instruction to advanced standards. Ideally, the centre should have facilities and courses for special groups, such as the elderly or the handicapped so that they can enjoy the opportunity of sport for all.

Key messages for the public include:

- The centre offers the opportunity to try out a wide variety of sports.
- The centre caters for people of all standards.
- Elderly or handicapped people have the opportunity to try the full range of sports.

EXAMPLE 9: INDUSTRIAL MATERIALS

Information on new industrial materials is aimed at designers, purchasing staff and senior executives.

Designers

The prime target is designers; they specify materials so they need to understand their properties and their applications. They are interested in the performance characteristics and the results that have already been achieved in their own or in other industries. If they are going to change specifications, they need to be convinced that the new material will help them achieve significant performance or reliability benefits.

Key messages for designers include:

- This material has been proven in the most demanding applications.
- The material has outstanding performance characteristics.
- The material has been successfully used in other industries.
- A comprehensive technical service supports the product.

Purchasing managers

Purchasing managers are interested in the cost effectiveness of the materials. They are not concerned with the performance of the material, but they need to understand the overall cost benefits – which might include better usage of materials, improved machining, reduced waste and savings on other manufacturing processes. Although the initial costs of the material may be higher, through-life costs should be lower.

Key messages for purchasing managers include:

- A material which reduces overall manufacturing costs.
- Minimal wastage saves on material costs.
- Cost-effective product.

Senior executives

Senior executives are interested in the business benefits of the new material. They need to understand how it can be built into a development programme that will improve product performance and build a competitive edge. If the enhanced product offers significant customer benefits, it can be seen as a marketing investment.

Key messages for senior executives include:

- Material will provide an enhanced product to improve market performance.
- Material will allow company to develop new products and enter new markets.

EXAMPLE 10: BUSINESS TELEPHONES

A telephone is a telephone, but the marketing approach differs between small and large businesses.

Small businesses

Small businesses need a cost-effective service that keeps their operating costs at a low level. They also need the facilities to integrate other telecommunications services, such as the fax or modem, which will grow with the business. Modern digital technology means that a standard telephone can carry out a whole range of functions that increase the flexibility of the business. Communications emphasize the improved response to customers and the way in which a business can be built around the telephone.

Key messages for small businesses include:

- Call cost rate is low.
- The telephone is part of an integrated communications system.
- Additional facilities can be added easily as the business grows.

Corporate sales

In large corporations the emphasis is on the sophistication and quality of the system and the levels of support that are provided to the customer. The integration of communications and information systems can help to increase the customer's competitive advantage. For example, if a company introduces a telephone-based customer response system, it can provide a higher level of customer service. However, to achieve that may take a high level of planning and consultation that only a capable telephone supplier can provide.

Key messages for this market include:

- Company provides complete communications systems.
- Complete range of customer support services.
- Communications systems can be used to build competitive advantage.

BUILDING KEY MESSAGES INTO COPY

Getting the key messages right again and again takes skill and consistency. It's no good having a powerful message and then changing it in every publication. Here are some extracts from a range of publications and presentations for a computer services company.

> We provide the full range of services and can tailor a specific service solution to meet your short- and long-term requirements.

> The right services are a vital ingredient in the successful application of information systems, so we provide a total solution – an integrated set of hardware and software products, support, system management, training, consultancy and user services.

These key messages are vital components of a brochure that provides a management overview of customer services. Here is the same message from a divisional director talking to a customer user group.

> But we recognize that each department has its own unique needs, perhaps with special software or networking requirements, so standard service may not be appropriate ... So the type of service we offer must be flexible and adaptable to change. It must be a total service solution so that all the elements are there. In other words, we must give you a range of service options.

Next, the key messages are used on a leaflet promoting the service available from a local branch.

> Through the South East branch we support your whole business, helping you to develop a competitive edge. You have wide-ranging service needs and we have the resources to meet those requirements.

Every product brochure contains the same key messages.

> Facilities management is part of our complete service.

The same message is turned on its head to ensure the salesforce understand the benefits of the total solution.

> Environmental services are part of our total services solution. This increases account control by putting all business through the account team, preventing competition developing.

Below, in an executive guide to partnership, the company puts the total solution in the context of the customer's business.

> If you want to improve the quality of your operations, you need to implement a total business solution. You need to relate your information systems strategy to your organization's business objectives and to ensure that all the elements are in position for a rapid and successful implementation.

These key messages are working hard for the services company. Every time they appear in a publication or presentation, they help to reinforce a consistent image about the company and that reassures the customer.

SUMMARY

Key messages are essential elements in copy. They ensure that customers and prospects get the most important messages about the product or service. However, the relative importance of the messages varies with the target audience. Although you may be writing about the same product, the key messages for a chief executive will be different from the key messages for a designer.

The process for developing key messages is:

- identify the decision makers;
- analyse their concerns or interests;
- select the benefits of the product or service that reflect those interests;
- include the key messages in every communication with the customer or prospect.

Chapter
TEN

PLANNING COPY CONTENT

When you plan copy content, make a list of all the information that needs to be included in a publication to persuade the prospect to make a decision. In a product brochure, for example, this would include key product benefits, information about the company and the positioning statements, which should be included in every publication.

HELPING OTHER PEOPLE TO EVALUATE YOUR WORK

The contents list is a method for planning and checking – it shows the people who approve your copy what you intend to say before you start writing in detail.

The contents list shows how you intend to present the argument for this product. Have you included all the information that is important, is it in the right order and is there a good balance between the sections?

The people who contribute to the project and those who evaluate can check your plan easily at this stage. All they have to do is comment on a list – add information or put the points in a different order. There is no need to worry about style or detail – that comes later.

STRUCTURING A CONTENTS LIST

A contents list should have a clear simple structure so that people can check it easily.

Using a numbered list

The simplest way to begin a contents list is to write down a series of numbers. You can then list the key points in a logical sequence or in order of importance.

This is a good technique for presenting complex arguments and it is also quite valuable for putting together scripts for presentations or videos.

Dividing a publication into sections

Alternatively, divide the publication into sections, using the number of pages or spreads as a basis. Then allocate the key points to each of these sections. There may be five sections or more. Put together a major statement for each section – it might be an important benefit or it might be one aspect of the argument.

EXAMPLES OF COPY CONTENT

A sales presentation

Here is an outline for a sales presentation on a new range of biscuits.

1. Here's a new range of biscuits that will boost sales over the Christmas period.
2. The biscuits fill a gap in the luxury biscuit sector. This sector has shown the strongest growth over the last five years and it is proving to be the highest volume sector over the Christmas period.
3. These biscuits contain the best selection of all competitive products.
4. They are premium priced at retail level to give a good profit margin.
5. There are three different pack sizes in the range to give your consumers a choice.
6. The products are attractively packed to have good shelf and consumer appeal.
7. They will be backed by a national advertising campaign and a promotional programme to encourage high levels of purchase.
8. This is part of a programme of continuous product development from this leading biscuit company.
9. Other products in our range include ...

The sales representative can use this to present a new range of products in a structured way. The list covers all the information that the retailer needs to evaluate the product. The list could easily be modified to change the emphasis in the presentation. It can also be adapted quickly to develop presentations for other product groups.

A brochure introducing a new model in the range

A new microwave cooker is launched on to the market with a consumer brochure. It is part of an existing range of microwaves.

1. Microwaves are now one of the favourite types of cooker. They're quick, convenient and give great results.
2. This model has a new feature – it browns off meat and casseroles to give a traditional appearance just like oven cooked.

3. This really increases its versatility and makes the food more appealing.
4. It also incorporates the latest weight defrost cook device which means you don't have to guess cooking times for perfect results.
5. Like all the microwaves in our range it has simple clear controls for easy operation.
6. It's also got our superb reputation for reliability plus the no-nonsense guarantee.
7. To help you get started we include a free recipe book.
8. This is one of our range of advanced domestic electrical appliances designed to make modern living easier.

This brochure is aimed at consumers who have already used a microwave and may be trading up and also at those who are buying one for the first time. The contents list begins by putting microwaves in context because some people may not be familiar with them. It introduces the new features because that's what creates the real interest, and then reassures the buyer with information about the traditional values of that manufacturer's products.

Introducing a new manufacturing concept

Take a look at the approach for a new computer-based manufacturing system. Successful implementation will require wide-ranging management changes in the customer company, so the copy has to lead the customer carefully.

1. Competitive conditions demand that we improve our manufacturing performance. The key indicators are delivery, quality and reliability plus cost.
2. A new manufacturing approach will help to do that by reducing the amount of work in progress and giving greater control over the whole process.
3. It provides benefits like reduced lead times, less stock, better response to customer demands, decreased costs and better profitability.
4. The issue is so important it should be discussed by the whole management team.
5. Marketing will have new opportunities.
6. Purchasing needs to change its relationship with suppliers.
7. Production and stock control need to understand the new technology and approach.

8. This is a complex issue but we have the experience to give impartial advice on it. We have already implemented it at our factories and we'll describe our experience in setting it up.

9. This will give you a blueprint for planning your own changeover.

10. The new approach involves extensive use of computers and communications with your customers and suppliers so that everyone knows what is happening. In some cases that means physical relocation to get closer together.

11. As a result stocks are much lower and they come when they're needed.

12. These are some of the figures we achieved at our factory.

13. This is the computer system we used to achieve it. It includes all the functions needed to plan, control and communicate in this manufacturing system.

14. It runs on existing hardware and you won't have to go through a major upheaval to install it.

15. It integrates with other products in our manufacturing range and provides the basis for a completely integrated approach to manufacturing.

16. We can advise with confidence because we're one of the most experienced suppliers to the manufacturing sector.

This brochure contains much more background and advice than a conventional product brochure. The aim is to educate the customer and build understanding before selling the product. The contents list builds confidence, provides advice and guidance and slips the product in almost unnoticed.

Introducing a new service

In this brochure a management consultancy is explaining why its new services are so important. It begins by explaining why the service is important and shows how the customer will be involved.

1. It's vital that companies get the right advice on their computer strategy.

2. We have the resources to identify your requirements and work with your management team to achieve them.

3. Because we've been so closely involved with your business strategy development we know how computers will fit into that.

4. We've had the experience of this strategic work with many large corporations and we're working with some of the most famous names in the business.

5. This is the way we handle the project. You select your own management team and we brief them on the decisions they have to make.
6. Here's an outline of the sort of decisions they will be making.
7. Then we work together on this computerized model which we have developed. We'll help you develop the right strategy.
8. We'll then give your management team a list of key tasks to carry out.
9. In the meantime they will have attended briefings and seminars on managing change so that they're fully prepared for the challenge.
10. This is one of a range of management services we provide to help support you in achieving your business objectives.
11. You'll find this is one of the best ways of building your business.

Once again this company is helping to build confidence in its customers and takes them forward by getting them deeply involved in the process. This contents list sets out a clear way forward for the client, showing what is required on both sides and it also demonstrates the professionalism of the consultancy.

SUMMARY

The contents list can be used to plan your copy before you get down to detailed writing. It helps to structure complex arguments and allows other people to contribute to the copywriting process in a constructive way.

Using a numbered list is a very simple way of planning content – putting the important information in order of importance or in a logical sequence.

Chapter ELEVEN

THE COPY BRIEF

A copy brief helps the writer to prepare copy. It must lay out the direction the copy is to take and provide all the information the writer needs to complete the copy. A good brief will be self-contained – the writer will not need any more information to begin, although he may wish to go into more detail on specific subjects.

BACKGROUND

The brief should begin with the background to the project:

- What is the overall aim of the project?
- What are the business threats and opportunities?
- Why is the publication being written?
- How does the publication fit into the overall marketing programme?
- Is it being used as part of a direct sales operation?
- Is it just background information for a more wide-ranging operation?

The background material should ensure that the publication works in context and is not written in isolation. The background would also list the other publications and communications that are being used to support this particular programme.

OBJECTIVES

The brief should then go through a series of objectives:

- What is the overall corporate objective?
- What is the marketing objective?

The overall communications objectives and the specific task for individual publications are derived from those objectives.

The objectives of the publication should be detailed, for example:

- convert 45 per cent of readers to action;
- ensure that senior managers understand the business objectives of this programme;
- raise awareness of this new service among existing customers.

COMPETITIVE INFORMATION

The brief also looks at the competitive situation:

- Who are the competitors providing a similar product or service?
- How do they rate compared with the company's product?

This can help the writer to identify some of the key benefits to be described. It also helps to show how other companies have tackled the problem of describing the product and provides a basis for information gathering.

PRODUCT INFORMATION

The product or service should be described in full detail:

- What is it?
- What is it used for?
- How does it operate?
- What are the main benefits to the customer?
- What are the advantages over competitive products?

Detailed product information should be available even though only part of it may be used in the actual text. The writer should also be aware of other sources of information. Any research on the product and how it has been received or perceived by the market will be useful in building an effective picture of the writing task.

TARGET AUDIENCE

The target audience should be covered in detail:

- What sort of companies buy the product?
- Which business sectors are they in?
- What size are these companies?
- Who are the main decision makers?

- What is their role in the decision-making process?
- What are their business concerns?
- What is their perception of the company and the product?

TARGET PERCEPTION

The writer should be aware of any positioning statements and key messages that are important to that product or service. The writer's task is not to invent the benefits of the product – that is a job for the marketing department – the task is to communicate those benefits as strongly as possible. The brief should also state the intended result of the brochure in terms of response or action.

MECHANICAL INFORMATION

It is important to know what the format is and how the copy will be used. In an illustrated brochure, the illustrations can be used to carry part of the message, together with headlines and subheads. The format also helps to give a structure to the copy. It shows how the argument can be broken down into a number of different sections.

APPROVAL OF THE BRIEF

The brief should be circulated to members of the group involved in briefing and approving the project. Once the brief has been approved, members should not be able to change it without good reason.

AN EXAMPLE OF A BRIEF

Here is an example of a copy brief.

Background

The company competes in the industrial market.

Currently it holds 12 per cent of the market but it is losing ground to competitors whose products are seen as more innovative and relevant to the needs of the market.

The company has therefore changed its focus and is currently conducting a survey to see what its customers really need.

The survey information will be used as the basis of an on-going communications programme that should increase sales of the company's products and help to generate additional revenue and long-term customer loyalty.

This provides information on the market and shows the context the copy will operate in. It shows the problems the company has to overcome and outlines the actions that are being taken. It also hints at the current and target perceptions although these will be described in more detail later.

Communications objectives

The copy must persuade the key decision makers that the company is now more concerned with customers' needs and is taking steps to remedy the situation.

It should show how the company is aiming at building a long-term partnership that will provide the customer with the best form of service.

The immediate task is to convince x per cent of decision makers that this new service is valuable.

This sets out what the copywriter has to achieve in precise terms and it does not get confused with broader marketing objectives.

Product information

This industrial service helps companies run their business effectively.

The service is much more closely aligned to customers' real needs so it helps them meet their business objectives.

It contains all the elements that are right for the business and it will provide the users with the means to improve their own performance.

The service is cost effective and priced to represent real value for money.

It is convenient because it can be delivered either on site or at a central location.

The company has an established reputation in this market.

The writer can use this information to build a profile of the product and organize the structure of the copy.

Target audience

The key decision makers are likely to be the owners or managers of smaller outlets, plus the staff who actually deal with this on a day-to-day basis.

They hold the budget and they have the discretion to make decisions.

In larger organizations, there is likely to be a specialist who deals with the project or alternatively it could be perceived as a strategic product and may be discussed by the board.

The key concerns of this target audience are as follows.

In the larger organizations, they will include developing the competitive edge, improving sales performance and productivity and making the best use of scarce resources.

The project specialist will be interested in the quality of service and the way in which it offers advantages over competitors.

In the smaller outlets, customers will be thinking about how to make the best use of their staff and how to get real value for money from their budgets.

This description of the target audience gives a good basis for the writer to procede because he now knows what he has to achieve.

Mechanical information

This will be a sixteen-page brochure that is broken down into a number of sections.

SUMMARY

The copy brief is an essential document. It gives the writer the information he needs to plan and write copy. The brief also helps to secure the agreement of all people who are involved in briefing and approving the project.

Part
TWO

WRITING TASKS

Chapter TWELVE

WRITING ABOUT PRODUCTS

●●

This first set of examples looks at the skills required to describe products in a number of marketing situations. Your task is not just to describe a product or service but to understand how that product information is used to achieve different marketing objectives. The copy approach will vary with each situation. We will look at the following:

- Launching a new product to the salesforce.
- Launching an innovative product.
- Adding value to commodity products.
- Branding high value products.
- Making consumer technology simple.
- Marketing training services.

LAUNCHING A NEW PRODUCT TO THE SALESFORCE

A company takes a significant financial risk when it launches a new product. It takes money to develop and produce it and the company is unsure at the outset how the market will receive it. A new product launch can be a traumatic event and good communications are vital. One of the most important writing tasks is to convince the salesforce that they can sell the product. The emphasis in the copy is on helping the salesforce to understand the new product and its benefits to them. A simple product description detailing the features and benefits of this product would not be enough.

An electrical goods company launches a new hi-fi system that incorporates the latest compact disc and audio technology and is priced at the top of the market. The company is best known for its budget audio systems, which are reliable and represent good value for money. The new product takes it out of this well-established position and is likely to cause a few surprises when it is announced.

Build enthusiasm

The most important task is to convince the salesforce – they have to persuade dealers to stock the product and encourage them to sell it. The product is launched at the annual sales conference with this presentation by the marketing director.

> We have a superb reputation for reliability and value for money. Our products have sold millions and we're now first choice in that market sector. But where do we go from here? Our consumers are changing, they're loyal to our products, but they're getting older and they're getting more affluent. They're looking to buy their next audio system.

Explain the market opportunities

The marketing director has set the scene for a product introduction. He wants the salesforce to understand that they are building on established success. They are not taking a leap in the dark. They will be selling products to consumers they understand.

> Until now we haven't had a high specification product to offer consumers, so we've been losing sales to companies that we don't regard as competitors. What we must do is protect our customer base because loyalty is the strongest weapon we've got. Consumers now want sophisticated products and, if we don't provide them, our competitors will.

This signals a change of direction for the company. Until now, they have concentrated on a specific product range – they have been a product-oriented company. They realize that they can sell additional products to the same consumers by building on their loyalty. Traditionally, they have seen sophisticated audio and hi-fi as a separate product group, but they realize that both products are bought by the same consumers.

> The problem is that most consumers and dealers perceive us as the company that produces reliable, value-for-money products. We're not seen as sophisticated or technically advanced and we haven't got hi-fi products. Well, now we have – the XY600ZW series for the next generation of audio enthusiasts.

Position the product

The marketing director has anticipated the problem. Consumers won't see the company in that market and they won't believe that they have the products. This could be worrying for the salesforce.

> We want to build on our core brand values. We don't want consumers to think that we've just put our label on somebody else's hi-fi system. We're positioning the XY600ZW as the value-for-money hi-fi system – the one

you can understand and trust. That first point is important because research shows most people feel uncertain when they buy hi-fi for the first time. They're confronted with technical detail. It's seen as an enthusiast's world where people talk a language of their own.

That reassures the salesforce – here is a product they and the consumers can understand and trust. More important, it gives the salesforce a benefit they can sell – accessibility. The company is widening the market for hi-fi, encouraging more consumers to come and try.

Help the salesforce sell the product

We can't compete on reliability alone in that market. We have to demonstrate technical competence and appear to be offering consumers a unique experience. We plan to limit distribution of the new range to a select group called the Hi-fi Studio. To participate, dealers must agree to send one of their staff on a special training course and stock a minimum quantity.

That's another plus for the salesforce. By limiting distribution and positioning the franchise as exclusive, their task of selling in to dealers becomes easier. The Hi-fi Studio label also tells consumers that the company now sells sophisticated products.

Explain the promotional support

To support your sales effort we'll be running a competition for dealers and consumers offering a block of tickets for a major concert plus a compact disc collection. The theme behind the competition is the quality of sound. It positions the new product and it's relevant. Dealers will have to answer questions about hi-fi quality based on information in the dealer guide and consumers will be entered in a free prize draw when they purchase the equipment. The competition will be promoted extensively on radio and in music stores where we have a tie-in arrangement.

Motivate the salesforce to sell the product

It's important to the salesforce that their sales effort is supported by promotional activity that is relevant. They prefer to sell products that consumers and dealers want; but they also like a personal incentive.

We haven't forgotten you, of course. There's a sales competition based on product knowledge and sales. First prize is a weekend for two in Berlin, home of one of the world's great orchestras, and there are runner-up prizes of compact disc collections.

The salesforce needs motivation to sell and to acquire the right level of product knowledge.

Summary

This is a presentation that could have been handled badly. The brief to the writer was to describe the benefits of the new product and the launch support programme. The scriptwriter understood the risks the company faced and planned his presentation script carefully to achieve a number of objectives.

- Build enthusiasm so that the salesforce are receptive to the new product.
- Explain the market opportunities so that they understand who will buy the new product and why.
- Position the product so that the salesforce understand how it will be seen by consumers and how it relates to the current product range.
- Help the salesforce sell the product by showing how it will be distributed.
- Motivate the salesforce to sell the product by providing a personal incentive to sell.

LAUNCHING AN INNOVATIVE PRODUCT

In the previous example, the presentation described a product new to the company, but not new to the market. Consumers were already familiar with sophisticated hi-fi systems. However, when a company introduces an innovative product, it may need to educate the market before the product is acceptable. This is because potential customers may not understand the product or its potential benefits, and they may not wish to take a risk. Product description needs to be backed by customer education.

Educate your customers

With a new material, for example, it may take a complete education programme to get designers to specify the product.

> This new product will help you achieve new standards of strength and lightness. It's a product that has been thoroughly tested and proven in the aerospace industry and now it's finding wider commercial application.

Designers will be taking a risk if they specify the material without some kind of documented evidence on its success and suitability. However, the fact that it has been widely used in the aerospace industry means that it must be worth considering.

Provide practical help on product usage

> To help you design with this new material, we'll be running product workshops on your premises and we'll provide you with a set of computer-

ized design guidelines. We'll also be offering a technical helpline and a free design evaluation service for the first six months of your contract with us.

This provides designers with reassurance and some really practical help on the best way to make use of the material. It is designed to reassure them that if they do use the material they will never be alone. The workshop is a clever idea for getting closer to the designers and helping them to make use of the product.

Help customers present products to their managers

You'll find you can save money through the whole life of the equipment by specifying this material. It reduces maintenance because it is so durable and that in turn improves the reputation for reliability.

This provides further ammunition for the designer when he has to argue with the purchasing or finance department because the material is at first sight more expensive then conventional materials. By helping the designer to overcome objections within his own company, the supplier is almost getting a free presentation to the decision makers he is not able to reach.

The new material can be machined and finished using conventional manufacturing materials. It does not require any special manufacturing techniques or special production training.

That comes as a relief to any designer who thought he might have to reorganize the production department to cope with the new material. Finally to help him convince the senior management team:

The new material will help your company develop a stronger market position by giving you access to new markets and providing you with even higher standards of performance and reliability.

This is not just a substitute material – it is one that can be used to build new product potential and that can give the designer a lot of credibility when he is presenting his proposals to the rest of the company.

Help your customers make informed decisions about your product

Other products may require a formal educational approach. When computers were in their infancy, the major suppliers spent a lot of time and effort on executive education so that their customers understood how to evaluate a sales proposal correctly.

Buying a new computer system is not simply a matter of deciding which is the most powerful processing system. Computerization can change your whole organization and that can have far-reaching management implications. For example, you'll need extensive training programmes to ensure your users can get the most out of their equipment quickly and you'll need to train your managers to make sure they know how to adapt their departments and their working practices to the new technology.

This explains to executives that they need to consider the full implications of a change to computerization. By providing their customers with comprehensive background information, the company knows that it will get a more informed purchasing decision and it will also build a dependent relationship before the proper sales process even begins.

> Our executive briefing sessions will enable you to look at the strategic implications of information technology away from the pressures of day-to-day decision making. The briefing centre is purpose built for executive action with seminar rooms and meeting rooms where you can share your concerns with fellow executives in confidence. It's conveniently situated near main communication centres but it's far enough away to keep you away from pressure.

Reassure your customers

Manufacturers of consumer products may need to run educational campaigns if they are to overcome people's natural resistance to change. For example, the health scare about microwave ovens just a short time after they were introduced could have quickly killed an emerging market. The manufacturers' response was to run a co-ordinated education campaign to make sure that any misconceptions were quickly corrected. Sometimes the argument can be turned on its head. When a company with a good reputation for fine filter coffees wanted to break into the instant coffee market it used tradition to educate the customers, using the slogan. 'Everything we know about coffee making in an instant.' This immediately elevates the coffee to a classic and gives the customer confidence. This company is unlikely to compromise its reputation for quality filter coffee by producing poor instant coffee, so the assumption is that it must be good.

Summary

New products and new technology do require a degree of confidence building before people will take the chance. Even then it's worth reassuring them that other people have got it right by making the correct choice. The phrase 'nobody ever got fired for buying IBM' is now a classic saying for people thinking about changing suppliers and a phrase like 'two thousand satisfied customers can't be wrong' helps to build the level of confidence.

- Educate your customers so that they understand the features and benefits of your product.

- Provide practical help on product usage so that customers can try out the product for themselves.

- Help customers present products to their managers; the prime contact in a customer organization may not be the only person making a decision, so help that contact to sell the product for you.

- Help your customers make informed decisions about your product – they may not understand the full implications of buying and using a new product.

- Reassure your customers that they are not taking a risk by buying a new product.

ADDING VALUE TO COMMODITY PRODUCTS

When products are established in the market-place and when there are many competitors offering similar products, it can be difficult for customers to distinguish between them.

For example, building products such as bricks, cement, timber, nails and paints rarely have a brand value. These are commodity products and price is often the main buying factor. Commodity products suppliers must build a brand around their name and show that they offer a better service to succeed.

Help your customers succeed

U-Build builders' merchants wanted to show that they were different; their strategy was to support professional builders with products and services that would help them complete a first-class job. The U-Build catalogue takes this concept further.

> U-Build recognize that a builder's reputation stands by the work that he does. After all a professional job finished in good time is his best advertisement. But to produce a high standard of work a builder needs a high standard of building materials. And he needs to know that he can get those materials when he wants them.

This introductory copy avoids the traditional opening of listing every product the company supplies and focuses on the builder's needs.

Stress price and quality

There's a reassurance on price too in the introduction because builders have to put in competitive tenders for their work.

> Because we're the region's biggest timber and builders' merchants, we've got an immense buying power which means that you benefit from highly competitive prices.

The emphasis though is on buying power not cheapness for its own sake because U-Build stake their reputation on quality. Quality and competitive prices are a valuable combination.

> We select only brands known for quality and reliability. All our products meet the very highest professional standards. They are manufactured by specialists who combine craftsmanship with the most advanced manufacturing techniques.

Offer advice and guidance

Most builders' merchants claim to have helpful staff, but U-Build staff have high levels of technical skill, and that gives the company a definite competitive advantage.

> U-Build offer computer-aided design for planning building installations. Just supply us with your requirements and using sophisticated computer techniques we will analyse your specification and determine the most economic design for each application ... The result is installations complying with all the building regulations and codes of practice. We can also offer a specialist consultancy service whereby our own system design experts are supported by structural engineers to undertake specialized design studies.

This specialist service provides a level of expertise that would normally be bought in as an extra service.

Guarantee product reliability

A good guarantee is a valuable promise to any builder who wants to promote his own workmanship.

> Our plants design to the highest standard as defined within BS 5268 and the manufacturing systems are quality assured in accordance with BS 5750.

Provide a broad product range

U-Build's reputation rests on supplying everything for the builder, not just commodities like bricks and timber. The catalogue achieves the highest standards of design and photography and it includes information on consumer products such as kitchens and bathrooms that a builder can use to show his customers. The style of copy changes to reflect this consumer role.

> Whatever the style, whatever the price range you're looking for, we have a kitchen to suit your needs. Most of our showrooms have a kitchen and bathroom showroom where kitchens are shown on display in room sets. Our Superior range features stylish continental design and quality construction.

Appeal to a wider market

The U-Build catalogue switches from consumer speak to builder's language when it is appropriate. This helps to broaden the appeal of the catalogue and ensures that U-Build can compete with the increasing number of do-it-yourself outlets. Here is some copy on tiles, for example, written for the consumer.

> We have a collection of co-ordinating wall tiles to complement the very latest in kitchen and bathroom designs.

And, for the builder who has to fix those tiles.

> U-Build offer a diverse range of additives, sealants, adhesives and mastics from many of the leading manufacturers in the industry, renowned for the quality and effectiveness of their products.

On doors, they move easily from one to the other.

> Doors today have become an important architectural and design feature in their own right – they can totally transform the look and character of the home ... And to reduce on-site costs further choose from our ready-glazed range featured in this catalogue – we can even supply doors tailored to receive your own furniture and fittings.

Summary

It is this balance between plain talking and promotional hype that makes the U-Build catalogue so flexible. It gives the builder all the information he needs but it can be easily given to the consumer as a guide to practical products that are high quality but can be specified without compromising the builder's reputation. Here are the key copy pointers.

- Help your customers succeed; by providing the right products and the right advice, the builders' merchants can improve customer loyalty.

- Stress price and quality. This helps to move the argument away from price promotion.

- Offer advice and guidance; this aspect of service can help the builder improve his own business.

- Guarantee product reliability so that customers can put their trust in the company.

- Provide a broad product range so that customers can get all their needs from a single source.

- Appeal to a wider market to take full advantage of the company's competitive advantage.

BRANDING HIGH VALUE PRODUCTS

The technique of branding is more common in consumer markets, and this example looks at the other end of the spectrum to commodity products – high value consumer and business products.

The secret of selling high value, high quality products through copy is to establish a brand personality which is presented consistently in all communications. Consumers of this type of product need to know that they are buying something special and they need to be reassured that they have bought something which is worth the large sum of money they have spent on it.

Establish a pedigree

A luxury product needs to have a luxury pedigree.

> This is a product that comes from one of the country's longest established manufacturers. Our products have been the first choice of discerning people for over 150 years and we are often seen as the example that other people follow. In fact our name has almost become symbolic with the product.

This immediately attaches a certain aura to the product.

Use endorsements to establish credibility

Celebrity endorsement is also a useful device in this market – this is quality by association and it can live independently of the product qualities. Unfortunately if the product doesn't live up to the reputation, Mr X might swear at it rather than by it.

Reassure customers that they have made the right choice

Customers need to be reassured that they have made the right choice. In the luxury goods market, it is likely that more product brochures are read after the sale than before it.

> The sweater is made in the traditional way by craftspeople using the finest local materials – wool from the sheep that feed on the lush grasslands of the south side of the hills. The colours come from the special dyes that are unique to this part of the country so it's unlikely that you'll ever come across another one the same.

Create exclusivity

Exclusivity counts for a lot in this market – making people feel they have bought something unique.

> A limited edition of this special design is being offered for a period of three months only.

That helps to raise the price enormously. It is also useful to surround the product with other trappings of exclusivity.

> This product is only available in selected outlets of the following exclusive stores.

The same principles can be carried over to the after sales service that is provided with the product.

> If your watch should ever need repair, you must bring it to one of our authorized agents – only they have the skills and experience to ensure that your watch is maintained in the finest possible condition. But we won't ask you to pay for the repairs, we expect our products to last.

How's that for a statement of confidence in the product?

Create separate identities within a range

Although the examples so far have referred to high value consumer products, the same techniques can be used to create a brand identity within a range. For example, the top of the range car models often come with their own identity and qualities.

> When you choose this model, you know you've arrived. Everything about it says success, but in an understated way. When you put in the real effort to achieve that you want to be taken away in style.

This is appealing to ambitious people who want their life-style and their purchases to reflect their success. Banks also have unsubtle ways of differentiating their customers.

> The gold card is your passport to financial freedom. You've shown us that you're responsible enough to manage your own affairs successfully, so we'll take off the spending limits because we know we can trust you. And if you want to arrange a loan we won't bore you with petty details, you can go straight to the front of the queue.

Compare this with the standards available to the average bank customer.

Offer customers a special level of service

This principle of differentiating services at the top end is just as rife in business-to-business markets.

> Gold service ensures that you have complete peace of mind. You'll have a personal account manager who is responsible for the quality of service in all aspects of our dealings with you. We'll include all the services you are likely to need in our online ordering service and we'll provide you with a regular reporting system that is tailored to the personal requirements of your company's management systems.

This shows that the company is concerned about its top customers and wants to recognise the importance of their business.

Add value to commodity products

Branding can also be used to prepare an identity for commodity products that would otherwise be sold at commodity prices.

> With the elite stationery service, we'll personally check your inventories every month and advise you when you need to replace your stock. What's more, we'll give you a detailed analysis of your stationery usage so that you can manage your business more effectively. As part of the opening package, we'll provide you with a set of executive stationery holders for your senior people, at no extra charge.

This is building an aura of speciality around a product that's very ordinary.

Offer customers special privileges

Privileged service can also be used to differentiate standard products from the competition.

> When you fly business class on our airline, you can be sure that you'll get all the service you need so that you arrive refreshed for the business. You'll get free business newspapers and magazines, a business briefing pack on the country you're flying to, plus of course a healthy business bite to keep you in check together with complimentary wines from some of the regions of your destination. You'll find it more convenient to fly business class – we provide a special departure lounge and we've cut down the check-in times so that you don't have to waste your valuable time queuing at a check-in. What's more if you fly regularly with us you'll qualify for a special frequent flyer's programme that provides you with some really valuable business gifts.

This is building a brand around quality service and special privileges for top customers.

Summary

Customers who buy high value products need to be reassured that they are buying something that is special and is worth the high cost. The copy must position products as exclusive, available only to a privileged few. Key copy tasks include:

- Establish a pedigree so that customers understand why the products are special.

- Use endorsements to establish credibility; customers like to feel they are in good company when they buy high value products.

- Reassure customers that they have made the right choice by providing them with comprehensive product information.

- Create exclusivity so that customers feel they have made a special choice.

- Create separate product identity within a range. This can help to segment the market by appealing to different groups of customers.
- Offer customers a special level of service to show that they are important to your business.
- Add value to commodity products so that they can be differentiated from the competition.
- Offer customers special privileges to encourage them to remain loyal to your products.

MAKING CONSUMER TECHNOLOGY SIMPLE

As the section on target markets showed, a business decision-making group would normally include at least one member who understands the technical performance of the product. This is not the case in consumer markets where individuals buy products.

Consumers can be impressed by technology or frightened by it. The market for audio products, for example, is clearly divided into people who want 'all the knobs' and people who simply want to play music without fuss. At the same time, the product should say high technology, even if it's easy to use. Anyone writing for this market has to tread a fine line between frightening people off and failing to impress them. Here is a brochure that manages to combine the best of both.

Present technology as a benefit

> This is the first of an exciting new generation of sophisticated, but simple to use video recorders that combine a wealth of technically advanced features and step-by-step programming that's as easy as ABC ... All the recorders feature HQ technology to give you the finest quality picture, while some of the range feature an indexer to help you find the beginning of a particular recording quickly and easily and a bar code scanning system that can simplify programming even further.

The consumer's overwhelming impression is that he is buying an advanced product – HQ circuitry, indexer, bar code scanning system. But it is approachable technology because it offers the consumer the benefit of simplicity – 'an indexer to help you find ... quickly and easily ... a bar code scanning system that can simplify programming even further'.

Explain the simplicity of using technology

To reassure the consumer even further, the brochure describes the programming process – a potential nightmare to anyone brought up in the pre-video age. How many adults still leave it to their children?

> It takes all the complexity out of programming the video: a series of simple step-by-step prompts guide you through each stage ... Now everyone in the family will be able to programme the video.

Everyone in the family presumably means parents! Phrases like 'simple step-by-step ... guides ... takes all the complexity out of programming' are deliberately included to build confidence. They can also compensate for over-enthusiastic showroom staff who try to sell on features alone without explaining the benefits.

Promise the consumer improved results

This approach to copy was built around consumer research that highlighted the benefits consumers felt were most important and that also revealed their concerns about using this type of equipment. Here's another brochure, this time on a video camera, that leads the novice gently through the labyrinth of technical features.

> As soon as you pick it up, you'll feel as confident as a professional. It's light, compact and easy to handle – just like holding an ordinary camera. You can concentrate on capturing the scene instead of struggling with settings and missing the action.

Anyone who has used an automatic camera – the point and shoot type – will understand the implications: 'just like holding an ordinary camera ... instead of struggling with settings'. But the promise is there: 'you'll feel as confident as a professional.'

> And everything is there in one unit; reliable battery power, so you've got no trailing power supply leads to worry about; a built-in condenser microphone for superb sound recording – no need for a separate cassette recorder.

This company is selling push-button technology, but it promises high quality results as well as simplicity.

> There's no complicated setting up or adjustments to carry out, and you don't have to worry about focusing or light conditions. Sophisticated video technology ensures the finest results automatically; HQ, that stands for High Quality, circuitry, a Pan Focus lens – no need to adjust the focus, and an automatic iris to match exposure to the light conditions. Indoors or out, whatever the weather, you're guaranteed great results.

Build confidence in technology

The technical explanation is dropped into that paragraph but it reinforces the benefits ... 'an automatic iris to match exposure to the light conditions'. However, the people who want 'all the knobs' can still impress their friends, 'It's got HQ circuitry and a Pan Focus lens.' It's the same with audio products.

> If you're buying a new stereo system, you want to enjoy it immediately. You don't want to be blinded by technology to get the best out of your system. With the compact, feature packed systems, just connect to the mains, plug in the speakers, sit back and enjoy the music. There's no need to worry about unsightly tangles of wire and cable because all the components are internally linked.

This is the system for people who don't want to be hi-fi buffs, but want the sound quality that is associated with hi-fi. Terms like 'immediately ... blinded by technology ... tangles of cables' provide that reassurance. Here is something for people who feel they ought to know about compact discs, but feel too embarrassed to ask.

> The first time you experience digital audio on compact disc, you'll realize what live music means. Terms like fidelity, purity of sound and brilliance at last take on real meaning. Digital audio brings you nearer to the reality of the original performance. It puts an end to the scratch and hiss you get on a vinyl record and the compact disc is durable enough to maintain that quality. Digital audio is the most exciting advance in home audio; it creates new standards in sound quality and it's now available at realistic prices.

Help consumers understand technology

People can be so confused by techno-speak that they shy away from buying a product or even discussing it with a salesperson because they feel inadequate or ignorant. This can be a real barrier to market growth for a technology product, so the sensible companies do their best to educate consumers and make their technology relevant. Research can be used to track the level of consumer awareness and understanding in the market-place to ensure that copy reflects current feelings. Video for example is now an accepted and familiar technology and so is microwave cooking, but when those products were launched, consumer education was extremely important.

Here is a simple explanation of the graphic equalizer for the non-technical.

> It produces a superb, controlled sound, fine tuned to your room. With the 5-band graphic equalizer, you can adjust the sound so that it's right for the music and right for your ear.

Summary

Technology can be a barrier to sales. If consumers do not understand a product, they may hesitate and choose an alternative that appears to be simpler and easier to use. Copy must reassure consumers that technology will benefit them and will not require advanced skills. The key messages are:

- Present technology as a benefit – show how it will improve the product or simplify its use.

- Explain the simplicity of using technology so that consumers feel confident they can use the product.
- Promise the consumer improved results – show that technology has a real practical value.
- Build confidence in technology. By making consumers feel they can benefit, they will be encouraged to try it.
- Help consumers understand technology – the more comfortable they feel, the easier it will be to sell them benefits.

MARKETING TRAINING SERVICES

You need different skills to write about services because the benefits of services are so different. Management training, for example, is an intangible service that has to be marketed at a strategic level. Training should bestow new skills and the ability to meet new challenges. But to understand why the training is relevant, it needs to be put in context.

This example is taken from the prospectus of a management training college, but the principles can be applied to any professional service.

Put training in the context of change

> 1993 is needed not just for inter-Europe trade, but to clear the managerial decks for the global business battles to come. Globalization and world class are not just business buzz words – they are the new reality. All this change means new pressures on managers. All of us have to learn new skills, face new challenges and turn old ways of doing things on their heads.

That sets the scene and should create a feeling of uncertainty. But help is at hand.

> The role of the Management Centre is to mirror the challenges ahead by constructing timely, informative added-value programmes that objectively meet the needs of today's manager. We have a series of highly topical practical programmes on how to manage your way to 1993 and beyond. We have a series of new programmes designed to face key global issues head on.

Establish credibility

This is an organization that aims to build confidence but they need to establish their own credibility.

> As the leading management development organization in Europe, we are committed to that role, a role we recognize as critical in these times of managerial change. Remember the Management Centre isn't just an organization that puts on programmes, we are very much a centre for management.

To reinforce their credibility, they introduce a series of courses for senior managers with a quote from a leading management writer:

> And the more experienced a manager becomes, the more productive and the more meaningful learning and management knowledge become.

Position the courses at a strategic level

The Top Management courses are creamed off from the rest of the course information. Each of the courses carries a title and a named speaker who has good credentials in management circles – they are positioned as seminars rather than just as training courses.

> They address issues of central importance including business strategy, corporate planning and aspects of marketing. There are also programmes which tackle organizational realities such as the difficulties of introducing change ... Our programmes provide an excellent opportunity for senior executives to learn new concepts, tools and techniques as well as challenge all too easily accepted assumptions. Managers are encouraged to rethink the usual approaches and to adopt novel approaches to enhance their problem-solving ability.

Relate training to customers' business objectives

Sometimes just pitching the management courses at the right level isn't enough. Training organizations need to get closer to the customer and explain how training will help improve business performance; in that way management training makes a contribution to the business.

> Management training has in recent years been under critical review. The results of formal management development programmes can be disappointing. The In-Company Training Group concentrates on the organization itself and on its real business problems, objectives and management development needs.

But in case delegates are concerned that these programmes will be of a lesser standard than the mainstream programmes.

> You may select a standard Management Centre programme from the catalogue and have it presented in your company taking into account your own business environment and areas of concern. The same public programmes can be more extensively tailored to your needs, with modules of the programme added, modified or withdrawn.

Build commitment to training inside the organisation

That was an example of the communications that would support the marketing of an external training service. Many companies operate their own internal training courses and they have to build commitment to them within the organization.

> The challenges of increased competition and rapid change have become the rule rather than the exception. Our future depends on all managers operating more effectively and incisively than our competitive counterparts. This requires changes in the company's strategies, culture and organization. The management training programme initially focused on education and awareness to create the common vision and attitude necessary for managers to tackle change. We now need to move on to face the challenges of the 1990s. As a member of the management team, you play a vital part in mobilizing and managing your team and the company's resources to meet these challenges.

This sets the scene for more detailed information on the training programmes. It helps to build commitment and understanding of the reasons for training and shows that it is built on a foundation of previous success.

> The challenge is to build on our successes to date and strengthen further our capabilities in ... quality, customer satisfaction, people management, logistics management and time to market.

Explain why training is relevant

Like their counterparts who take on external training, managers might claim that they don't have the time to attend courses that may not be entirely relevant. The promise is there.

> The programme provides you with the skills and knowledge you need to fulfil your role. This is achieved through a careful combination of intensive courses, practical workshops, strategic briefings and individual open learning modules ... consolidated by ongoing experience in your working environment.

This text is relating the courses to day-to-day tasks and making the training more relevant.

> Putting an end to 'going off on a course', every element of the programme is integrated with day-to-day business practices and is an integral part of improving personal and corporate performance. Unlike external events and isolated one-off courses, the management programme focuses specifically on managing in the company.

Describe tangible results

Training is more relevant if it promises specific results; this is what the manager will achieve:

- turning the company's strategies into action;

- managing effectively in the company environment;
- integrating course information into normal everyday practice;
- optimizing the company's resources;
- providing integrated solutions from multiple sources through a consistent company-wide approach;
- exploiting and managing change in a rapidly changing environment.

Summary

Marketing a service is not like marketing a product. The customer has nothing tangible to touch. It is therefore essential to relate training and other professional services to issues that are familiar and relevant to the customer – dealing with change or improving business performance. Most important, training, like other services, should promise tangible results. Key copy content includes:

- Put training in the context of change – make it relevant to the challenges customers face.
- Establish credibility; customers will respect an organization that has a reputation for success.
- Position courses at a strategic level; training should be seen as vital to business success.
- Relate training to customers' business objectives. Wherever possible, identify business processes that can be improved.
- Build commitment to training inside the organization by explaining how people can improve their own performance and contribution to a business.
- Explain why training is relevant; show how it relates to day-to-day tasks.
- Describe tangible results so that customers can see what they will achieve.

Chapter
THIRTEEN

WRITING ABOUT MARKET DEVELOPMENT

●●●

These examples look at the skills required to write publications that help to improve marketing performance by building understanding or supporting direct sales.

Your task is to change attitudes and provide information that will build understanding, awareness and commitment. We will look at the following examples:

- Dealing with new market opportunities.
- Appealing to different segments of the market.
- Helping customers use your products.
- Building understanding of services.
- Overcoming salesforce resistance.
- Building customer loyalty through dealerships.
- Selling a sales programme to retailers.

DEALING WITH A NEW MARKET OPPORTUNITY

When a new market opportunity arises, it's important to let people in the field know what the opportunities are and how best to meet them before competitors have a chance to catch up. The market opportunity can arise in a number of ways – because of new legislation, changes in product specification or changes in the competitive climate. It is important to provide sales staff with a clear understanding of the business opportunity, together with a practical action plan for making the most of the opportunity.

Help customers deal with the challenge

New legislation can often be the trigger. For example, the Environmental Protection Act meant that companies carrying on potentially damaging activities had to deal with complex new legislation. This gave companies who supply environmental products new opportunities.

> From next year, you will have to comply with tough new legislation and cut your emission levels by 10 per cent. To help you understand the new requirements, we will provide you with free advice and a handbook that gives you step-by-step guidance on meeting the legislation. Our Mark 2 extractor is designed to comply with all the requirements of the new legislation and, to make sure it's suitable for your building, we're offering a free design and installation service.

This copy recognizes that customers may not be fully aware of the new legislation, so it offers helpful advice as well as products and services to deal with the problem.

Reduce customers' uncertainty

In this type of situation there is often uncertainty and a great deal of confusion – any company that can demonstrate understanding of the problems can position itself as an authority and appear as a problem solver.

> We helped to draft the advisory legislation and we have been running seminars for local councils around the country on the impact of the new legislation.

Make sales staff aware of opportunities

Here is a company the customer can work with confidently. It is also important to get dealers and the salesforce familiar with the new situation so that they know how to approach the opportunity.

> Changes in MOT test legislation mean that there will be a great increase in demand for tyres. The new minimum tread depths mean that overnight millions of tyres will become illegal. That presents you with a great opportunity to build a wholesale tyre business. Get in touch with MOT centres and independent garages. Make sure they understand the implications of the new legislation and make them familiar with the service you offer.

Provide an action plan

This is building awareness of the opportunity and recommending a course of action. Tell sales staff about the level of service they will have to provide.

> This means that retail outlets will be looking for quick delivery of tyres to suit many different types of vehicle. You will need to hold stocks to cover a particular workload and you need to be able to get odd sizes quickly so that you can build a reputation for reliability. To help you achieve this, we have made an arrangement with a leading tyre network and they will provide you with the right level of stocking service.

Help sales staff sell the new service

Don't forget to help dealers to sell the new service by offering guidance on market opportunities and providing the right level of support.

> We have developed a package that will help you compete head on with specialist competitors. The package allows you to sell tyres from your existing workshop with minimum outlay on stock and equipment. We'll provide you with a step-by-step guide to marketing the new services. This will include an invitation to a seminar with technical experts which can help to build confidence in your customers. There's an information pack which you can leave with customers and we'll mail out an introductory letter to all the likely prospects. We'll also provide a free training service for your sales staff to make sure they are familiar with the requirements of the new legislation.

Building an incentive into the programme will make sure that sales staff achieve the launch targets.

> We're making a special introductory offer on your initial purchases and you'll be able to qualify for the sales competition by taking part in a product knowledge quiz.

Keep sales staff up to date with competitive activity

It is important to deal quickly with changes in the competitive climate. For example, if a competitor goes out of business or introduces a new product, that changes the balance in the market-place. Sales people need to know quickly so that they can take advantage of the opportunity.

> *Product alert:* one of our major competitors has withdrawn from the market because of financial difficulties. This means that we can now increase our market share and develop contact with a broader range of customers. We'll be letting you have a list of competitive accounts together with any information we have on their purchases and the products they sell. We need to take action quickly because this product range is vital to the industrial process and our other competitors will not be slow in going after this business.

Summary

This kind of new business bulletin is a common element of salesforce communications and – used properly – can be a very effective way of building new business opportunities. It needs to be handled carefully because too many over-hyped opportunities can lead to cynicism and a disregard of the really important challenges. Communications should provide sales staff with a clear understanding of the business opportunity, together with a practical action plan for making the most of the opportunity. The main communications tasks include:

- Help customers deal with new challenges by providing practical advice and guidance.
- Reduce customers' uncertainty about new business issues by positioning the company as an authority.
- Make sales staff aware of the opportunities; explain the background and the actions that need to be taken.
- Provide an action plan so that sales staff understand their responsibilities.
- Help sales staff sell the new service by providing guidance and support.
- Keep sales staff up to date with competitive activity so that they can respond quickly to opportunities.

APPEALING TO DIFFERENT SEGMENTS OF THE MARKET

When a product is well established, it can prove difficult to stimulate new sales. In the early stages of a new product launch, customer education and awareness-building campaigns help to stimulate consumer interest and sales gradually increase as the product is accepted. But it can be difficult to sustain growth after this initial period. One approach is to look at the needs of different sectors of the market. If there are sufficient differences, the market can be segmented with a range of models or product options to appeal to the different sectors. It is important that you understand these differences and reflect them in your copy.

Early growth in the market

This was the case with microwave ovens – as consumers became more familiar with them, their confidence grew and sales increased. At the same time, food manufacturers developed more and more products formulated for microwave cooking. This made microwave cooking more acceptable and suited the contemporary life-style, so there was a period of accelerated growth. Microwave sales lived off microwave food advertising and the process of customer education became unnecessary.

Identify the needs of different consumers

However, when sales began to level off, manufacturers had to look for other opportunities to build new sales. Product reliability was good, so the natural replacement cycle grew much longer – the industry was a victim of its own success. But by looking closely at the needs of different groups of consumers the manufacturers were able to identify opportunities to offer consumers a choice of additional benefits and encouraged them to buy a new model.

Add different functions to the product

For example, by adding automatic defrosting and a grill, the manufacturers were able to offer two products in one. This appealed to consumers who wanted more flexibility from their microwave. It also added even greater convenience and speed to the cooking process.

> This popular microwave offers a number of popular features – automatic cooking and automatic defrosting will do most of the thinking for you while the instant heat of the integral grill finishes the food to perfection. With so many features, it's ideal for most families.

Make the product simpler to use

Another model took the guesswork and planning out of microwave cooking by incorporating controls that asked the consumer to identify the product – the control mechanism selected the time and the temperature, rather like an automatic camera.

> This microwave has a unique sensing function. You don't have to weigh the food or work out the cooking time and temperature. Just key in the food category and the sensing mechanism will do the rest.

You can almost feel the sense of relief from people who are concerned at the apparent complexity of microwave technology. This model is aimed at a group of consumers who may not have tried microwave cooking before and it helps to broaden the market appeal of the product.

Add more sophistication to the product

Another variant combined conventional convected heat, microwave and grill to provide a versatile oven that gave consumers real choice and control in their cooking. That appeals to a group of consumers who have already experienced microwave cooking but may have been disappointed by some of the results.

> This microwave oven has a grill – you can give pies, joints and cakes the same crisp brown topping you get from a conventional oven. Use microwave technology to cook quickly and then add the finishing touch.

Summary

Manufacturers can segment a market by offering consumers a choice of models that meet their individual requirements. It can be difficult to communicate to consumers that they have this degree of choice. When they walk into a showroom, they see a series of white, brown or chrome boxes, all of a similar shape and all with lots of bewildering knobs or push-button controls. By focusing on the unique benefits of each model, a manufacturer can attract the right target audience.

- Identify the needs of different consumers; before you write the copy, you should be aware of the way the market is being segmented.

- Add different functions to the product. Concentrate on the additional features so that consumers feel they are getting value for money.

- Make the product simpler to use. As the section on making consumer technology simple showed (pp. 105–8), consumers will buy when they feel comfortable with new technology.

- Add more sophistication to the product to appeal to the consumer who is already familiar with the product, but may be looking for improved functionality.

HELPING CUSTOMERS TO USE YOUR PRODUCTS

One way to build customer satisfaction is to ensure that customers can make full use of your products, whether they are consumer products, services or business-to-business products. For example, the proud new car owner will feel less than happy if he hasn't got enough information to tune the radio or operate the basic instruments. Unfortunately, information like this is often left to the technical department, and unless it is well presented it will fail to contribute to the overall ownership experience.

Provide clear instructions

> Welcome to your new car. We hope you're enjoying the first few minutes' driving experience. Before you go too far, we suggest you try out the basic controls. We'll take you quickly through a start-up sequence and if there is something you don't understand you'll find full illustrated information in your owner's guide. If you're still uncertain, ask your sales representative or one of the dealer staff. We want to ensure that you're really satisfied from the moment you take possession of your new car.

This is part of an audio tape that is left in the cassette player of a number of new cars. It helps the new owner quickly get familiar with the car. It explains where to get further information when it's needed and it reinforces the message that the company really cares about the customer's well being.

Explain how to get the best use from the product

Here's another example, this time from a maker of power tools. This text is encouraging the buyer to make full use of the drill and show that it really was a worthwhile purchase.

> We'll sure you'll want to get the most from your new power drill, so please take the time to read the instructions and try out the basic functions on a

piece of test wood. If you're not sure about some of the controls, pop down to your dealer and ask for a demonstration. You can do that any day of the week, and you'll find that on Wednesday evenings there's a power drill workshop where a qualified woodworker will show new and experienced users how to get the most from their drills. If you plan to use your drill for home improvement projects, please send for our free leaflet on drilling tips around the home or send us an order for our illustrated book of home improvement projects, 'Getting the bit between your teeth'. If you have any queries about your drill's performance, call your dealer or telephone our customer hotline, any time up to midnight, seven days a week.

Of course, the instructions should be clearly written but, if there are queries, this friendly introduction tells the user where to get further information. Most people have experienced the unwanted product that lies unused simply because they don't know what to do with it. Helping them goes a long way to building real satisfaction. As well as building customer satisfaction, this introduction is building loyalty to the manufacturer and encouraging contact with the dealer – both activities that support long-term sales success.

Encourage people to try a product or service

This is an extract from a guide to legal services that explains how solicitors can help people understand how to get help with important day-to-day legal matters. The guide is helping to break down the barriers that surround the legal profession and encouraging people to find out more about their services.

If you haven't used a solicitor before, you'll be surprised how many ways we can help you. If you're buying a house or moving, we'll take care of all the legal details for you – we charge a set fee and you'll find full details in our leaflet, 'Moving home'. Maybe you're in dispute, with a neighbour, another motorist, your employer or your partner. We can give you advice on the best way to proceed and if necessary we'll act on your behalf.

Support your customers

In business communications, there is a strong emphasis on helping customers get the best possible results from products. Purchases have to pay their way quickly and the onus is on the manufacturer to support the customer in his use of the product.

To make the most of your investment in the new manufacturing system, we recommend that you implement a comprehensive training programme at a number of different levels. Your senior executives can attend our strategy course where they will gain an insight into the business development opportunities available. Departmental managers can attend the briefing sessions on the implications of the new system on their working practices so that they will get a better understanding of the management tasks facing them. The staff who operate the equipment on a day-to-day basis will be able to get full training on your own site so that they can become operational at the earliest possible opportunity.

Training is the most obvious example of the support that can be given to a business customer, but there are other activities such as management guides and seminars that can be used to increase understanding and awareness.

> We have the strategic ability to work with your executive team to determine the future direction of your business over the next five years. We support that consultancy with an implementation and project management service that ensures all the actions take place which are vital to the successful implementation of the project. We want to make sure that your company is equipped for success and that it fully understands all the implications of managing change.

This is from a management consultancy that wants to make sure its recommendations are implemented successfully. If it does not develop the right attitude in the customer there is a chance that the customer will not get all the benefits and the project could fail.

Summary

Helping customers make use of products reduces frustration and helps to build customer satisfaction. Clear instructions, advice on where to get further information and support services can be used to ensure the customer gets the best from a product or service.

- Provide clear instructions; if customers cannot use the product they will quickly be disappointed.
- Explain how to get the best use from the product; this increases the level of satisfaction even further.
- Encourage people to try a product or service. Good introductory material can build understanding and awareness.
- Support your customers by providing training and other services that help them to make effective use of your product in the shortest possible time.

BUILDING UNDERSTANDING OF SERVICES

Part of the process of market development is educating customers so that they are receptive to product information. For example, one of the biggest barriers to selling services is getting customers to understand the importance of services and why they need them. The problem is that many services can be avoided and they do not produce tangible results. Even routine maintenance can be avoided, as car manufacturers and dealers know to their cost. Your task is to write copy which explains why services are important and demonstrates their real benefit.

Offer customers peace of mind

> Regular scheduled maintenance is vital from a safety and economy point of view. It's essential that someone with skill and experience checks all the critical parts of your car so that you can enjoy miles of carefree motoring. By keeping your engine in tune, you'll save money on petrol because your car will be running more efficiently. And by catching those parts that are worn before they go too far you can avoid unexpected repair bills and damage to other components.

This is trying to convince unenthusiastic car owners that it really is worth spending money on regular servicing. The benefits are peace of mind and potential savings on running costs.

Help customers make better use of their own resources

Here is an example of a company offering its engineering services to clients to supplement their own resources.

> By using our design and development resources, you can improve your own product development programmes. We have experts on technology and manufacturing control who can work with your own development team members to supplement your own skills. Alternatively we can take on complete projects and provide you with a completely developed solution. That way, you won't have to commit any of your staff and they can concentrate on your own core business activities. We've got fully equipped laboratory and test facilities which your team can use and we have computer-based analytic facilities which you can use to monitor your own programmes.

This approach is ideal for a 'substitute service' where a company buys in scarce skills and resources from a third party, rather than hire additional specialists.

Educate customers about new services

You may be offering a service that is essential to a customer's business success, but which is not widely understood. This copy is introducing computer disaster management services.

> According to industry surveys, it has been estimated that around one in a thousand organizations are likely to suffer a computer disaster. Their computing facilities could be unavailable for a period of time and this threatens their ability to survive. The survey also reports that ninety per cent of all companies that have suffered a disaster and had no recovery plan subsequently went out of business.

This introduction uses an industry survey to give authority and credibility to the claim that customers must treat this issue seriously. If the supplier had opened with claims about the quality of their service most customers would have disregarded the issue as unimportant.

> Disaster survival is a business issue because information technology is now closely integrated with essential business and service operations to maintain competitive edge and efficiency. Successful provision against a disaster is essential for continued profitability and possibly survival.

Offer customers the benefit of your accumulated experience

This company explains the factors that have made its card processing business successful. The company explains that the experience they have gained in building that business could be important to other customers and they are offering that experience through their consultancy services.

> If effective customer programmes are important to your long-term business objectives, we'll work in partnership with you to build and maintain relationships through strategic marketing programmes.

The copy is trying to help the customer realize that customer and supplier share the same challenges and business objectives. That's a good basis for a partnership relationship.

> We have already proved through our business that strategic marketing programmes need to be backed by the right support and customer services, efficient administration and account management, data communications and management reporting.

This outlines the services that will be vital to the customer as well. Finally, the company builds in information on its own capability to deliver those services.

> This wide-ranging approach ensures that we can provide our customers with the experience, the market knowledge and the resources to launch, operate and manage dynamic marketing programmes.

The company has moved its customers through a well-planned sequence – identifying its problems, showing how the company's services can provide the solution, and demonstrating its own capability.

Help your customers identify their own problems

Helping customers identify their own problems is essential for two reasons – first, customers may not realize that they have a problem or an opportunity; second, they may not understand what sort of services are available and how they relate to their business problems.

The scenario is a useful way of dealing with this problem. The scenario focuses on the customer's business and problems, demonstrating that there is an understanding between the two parties.

> You want your staff to take pride in their equipment so that they are more careful in the way they use it.

This restates the customer's problem.

> The visits to your site are held during normal office hours so that your staff can see the work being done.

This is how the company responds to the customers' scenario.

> You want to make your staff realize that they are working for a caring organization ... The service will ensure that your equipment is kept in the best possible condition, improving the working environment and demonstrating that yours is a caring organization.

The company has demonstrated that it can identify with its customers' business objectives and provide services to meet them.

Summary

Because services provide intangible services, it can be difficult to convince customers that they are important. The copy must concentrate on helping customers understand the real benefits:

- Offer customers peace of mind – reassurance can be a powerful motivating factor.

- Help customers make better use of their own resources. The pressure to reduce internal costs and resources means that external services can provide a cost-effective alternative to employing additional staff.

- Educate customers about new services – they may not be aware of their own problems!

- Offer customers the benefit of your accumulated experience; by using your skills they can move their business forward.

- Help customers identify their own problems. Before customers understand your services, they have to be able to recognize their own needs. Use examples from their business to establish the importance of your services.

OVERCOMING SALESFORCE RESISTANCE

This aspect of market development ensures that the salesforce are committed to selling the product. Sales people sometimes object to certain products and

Writing about market development / 123

services that they are not keen to sell. For example, if a company normally sells high value capital equipment such as machine tools or computers, but then introduces a range of lower value services, they may encounter sales resistance. The salesforce argue that they are difficult to understand and time consuming to sell and give them little material reward. Your task is to explain the benefits of the new product or service in terms that reflect the interests of the salesforce.

Demonstrate account control

Sales people want to be able to keep tight control on their customers and any actions that help them to achieve that will be welcome.

> These services are vital to the control of our business. They help us maintain contact with customers we can't normally reach and they give us an ideal opportunity to build effective long-term relations with our customers. We have identified that customers rely on technical support for their machines, but they can no longer afford to retain their own staff. This gives us a unique opportunity to sell them a range of services and to get closely involved with their organization.

This is setting the scene for the salesforce telling them that there is a real opportunity there and encouraging them to get involved. It's important to stress the real benefits to the salesforce and to do this in concrete terms.

Help to build relationships

> To provide this service we'll be putting three engineers on site on a permanent basis and that is an excellent opportunity to get closer to the customer. Experience has shown that this is an ideal way – customers trust engineers and people on site can help to provide us with valuable information on the way the business is going. They have access to customer information that you wouldn't normally be able to get hold of. What's more, in presenting the service, you'll be talking to key executives and helping them plan their support strategy. This gives us a contact that isn't normally available and will enable you to build relationships at a much higher level.

This is pointing out the intangible benefits of the services and demonstrating that there is more to service sales than just the short-term financial rewards. The opportunity for contact and information is an important aspect of business-to-business marketing. It is also vital to show just how essential this is to the competitive environment.

Dealing with competitive threats

> Services can help to keep our competitors at bay because the last thing we want is a service engineer on site from another company. They can undermine customers' confidence in our products and can rapidly erode

our account control with other services. The other thing we have to watch is that services now represent a significant and growing part of our business. If we lose control over that, then we may see an attack on our profit and revenue and that will not help us to build our business. It's vital that we retain our control at this level because when our contract comes up for review we may find our position threatened.

Summary

Building salesforce commitment is an important part of salesforce communications. The task is more difficult when the salesforce do not understand why they have to sell certain products or services. The communications should concentrate on these issues:

- Demonstrating account control will encourage the salesforce to sell the products or services, regardless of value.

- Helping to build relationships. This is one of the most important tasks for the salesforce. Explain how the product or service will open doors for the salesforce.

- Dealing with competitive threats. Show how the product or service will protect the company's position and reduce competitive threats.

BUILDING CUSTOMER LOYALTY THROUGH DEALERSHIPS

Building customer loyalty is an essential part of long-term market development. If customers are satisfied with all aspects of a product and its related services, the company is likely to enjoy a high level of repeat purchase. In the car industry, for example, customers purchase new cars every two to three years and that leaves a long time for customers to be influenced by competitors. After-sales service provides the opportunity to maintain contact, build the highest levels of customer satisfaction and retain loyalty. While the manufacturers concentrate their efforts on getting the quality of the product right, the quality of after-sales service depends directly on the performance of the distributor. Your task is to ensure that distributors understand their role in building customer loyalty.

Tell dealers about customer expectations

A luxury car manufacturer defined the role of the dealer as 'delivering customer delight'.

> Owning one of our cars must be a memorable experience at all levels – not just at the point of purchase, but throughout the period of ownership in all aspects of the relationship between customer and dealer. It is essential that

… we deliver customer expectations at all levels – sales, after-sales and throughout the period of ownership … Dealership performance will be stimulated over time by a vigorous manpower development programme. Total commitment to training and development will produce better quality people at all levels from newly recruited trainees to dealer principals.

This statement shows the way ahead and indicates the way the result will be achieved. It is easy to express platitudes without providing practical guidelines. Another manufacturer takes a similar approach by telling their dealers what customers want and showing them how to achieve it.

Extensive market research into the car buying process from the customer's perspective has clearly identified a major opportunity to achieve differentiation in the areas of environment, branding, service, clarity of offer and convenience.

By quoting independent research, the company shows that this is an issue to be taken seriously.

The overall conclusion from all our market research is that customers expect a welcoming environment with a clear range of products and services on offer and a friendly reliable and trustworthy service at all times which meets their needs, thereby offering quality, value and convenience.

Give dealers practical guidelines

The guide then goes on to address specific actions that dealers can take to improve their customer satisfaction performance. Here a specific activity – offering customers courtesy cars – is positioned within the overall programme.

The courtesy car programme is a major step in building customer satisfaction and loyalty to our dealers. The programme responds to the changing levels of customer expectations and overcomes a major customer concern – inconvenience. This programme complements other dealer activities and is a further step towards building the highest levels of customer satisfaction.

This helps to put individual business programmes into perspective and ensures that dealers are continually reminded of the overall programme.

Involve everyone in the programme

This proposal for a corporate communications programme demonstrates the importance of customer care.

The aftermarket is now one of the most fiercely contested areas of the automotive market because it provides the key to customer loyalty and repeat sales. The success of our parts and service operations in implementing an effective customer care programme plays a critical part in our long-term marketing strategy. Through our parts and service operations we achieve some 75 million customer contacts compared with the 1.5 million vehicle sales which take place. This level of contact provides an excellent opportunity to get closer to the customer and demonstrate leadership in customer care.

Those figures really bring home how important the dealership is but, as the proposal warns, 'unless everyone within the dealer network is aware of the programme and committed to its success, it will be a missed opportunity'. To emphasize this even further, one manufacturer renamed its service training college 'The Care Institute'. That's a radical change for a college that concentrates on hands-on technical training for fitters and supervisors.

Relate customer care to individual jobs

It is this concentration on the nuts and bolts of customer care that really makes a programme work. Here's an extract from a customer satisfaction manual that uses quotes from customers as a starting point for remedial action.

> 'He'd made up his mind what he wanted to sell me and it took a long time to get him to understand that I wanted something else.'

> 'What a chauvinist! Just because I'm a woman he talked about a nice little runaround for the shopping and getting the kids from school.'

> 'I wouldn't go there again. The salesman did a real pressure selling job on me.'

These are situations that most sales people will be familiar with, but instead of hearing it from the sales manager, they're getting it directly from the customer because these are quotes taken from customer surveys.

Encourage action

The guide then follows up with practical advice from dealers who have dealt with that kind of problem.

> 'I make sure all my salesmen know my attitude – that the secret of our future success is getting customers for life.'

> 'I often contact customers a few days after delivery to check everything is OK. I make a point of talking to them about how we look after them – some of the points they raise are so simple and easy to correct.'

The section concludes with an action checklist to help dealers develop their own plans.

- Do the selling methods in your dealership encourage customer care?
- Do any of your staff need training?

- How can you ensure that your salespeople maintain contact with your customers?

Acknowledge dealership achievement

Many car manufacturers use incentive programmes to acknowledge dealers who achieve the highest standards of customer satisfaction.

> This is the most prestigious dealer programme in Europe and the winning dealers are indeed to be acclaimed. If you were not one of this year's award winners, I urge you to continue your efforts to maximize customer satisfaction and to strive to be amongst those who receive an award next year. No one, and that includes the winners, should ever lose sight of the issue of customer satisfaction which is fundamental to the future of our business.

The language of this statement is strong. In fact, it's almost overwritten, but that helps to elevate customer satisfaction to a strategic issue that's important to the company's most senior European executive. Its aim is to build commitment from the top.

Summary

To make a customer loyalty programme work, a manufacturer must encourage dealers to make a continuous effort to build customer satisfaction over a long period of time. Customer loyalty should be communicated in terms of practical actions, not expressed as platitudes about customer care. Key communications tasks include:

- Tell dealers about customer expectations; quote research or actual comments about customers' views of their service.

- Give dealers practical guidelines that enable them to operate customer loyalty programmes in their territory.

- Involve everyone in the programme. Customer satisfaction and loyalty is not just the responsibility of management; everyone affects a customer in some way.

- Relate customer satisfaction to individual jobs; this helps every member of staff understand how they affect the customer and what they can do to improve loyalty.

- Encourage action to ensure that dealers put a programme into effect.

- Recognize dealership achievements; incentive programmes encourage dealers to aim at the highest standards.

SELLING A SALES PROGRAMME TO RETAILERS

In certain markets, retail performance can be critical to overall market success. Companies help their retailers improve their business performance by operating business programmes to achieve specific results. For retailers to benefit from this type of programme, they need clear guidelines on the aims and operation of the programme. Here is an example of an extended warranty programme that is designed to retain dealership customers.

The programme guide is divided into five sections:

1. Description of the programme.
2. Benefits to the consumer.
3. Business benefits.
4. Selling the service.
5. Operating the programme.

Describe the programme

Tell retailers what the programme covers; explain its scope and tell them where they can get further information.

> This extended warranty gives customers a further two years' protection against unexpected repair bills. You can provide an assurance that breakdowns on components covered by the programme will be repaired free of charge. You will find details of the programme in the warranty manual which you will receive shortly.

Explain the benefits to the consumer

This section should explain to retailers how the programme will benefit their customers. This will build commitment to the programme and encourage retailers to sell it.

> The programme is regularly enhanced to increase customer benefits and provides a range of other benefits beyond mere warranty cover. For example, your customers will enjoy greater peace of mind, they will save money on large repairs and their car will have a higher resale value because it carries a watertight guarantee.

Show how the programme benefits the retailer

The main benefit of a programme like this is that it helps to improve the retailer's own business performance. If retailers understand those business benefits, they are more likely to participate in the programme. The main benefit of any programme is that it should increase profitability and improve customer loyalty. Here are a range of benefits that might be relevant to different programmes:

> The programme offers high profit opportunities, equivalent to the profit on the original sale... It builds long-term customer loyalty through a long-term servicing commitment, stronger links through the ownership cycle and a closer relationship between the customer and the service department. The programme will increase service revenue over later years of ownership... It will build repeat service business helping to stabilize the service department and improve business planning.

Provide guidelines on promoting the programme

This section tells retailers about the marketing support available so that they can promote the programme effectively. It should describe the type of support material, how it is used and where it can be obtained. Good guides don't just put the material in retailers' hands, they explain how to make the best use of the material. Sales staff perform even better when they have guidelines on selling the product. This section of the guide should identify the sales opportunities, key customers, and sales techniques.

> There are many different opportunities to sell the warranty to your customers: when you are selling the new product, when you follow up after the sale, when the customer brings the product back for its first service, or when repairs are carried out.

It also explains who should sell the service – and that may not always be the sales staff.

> Service staff are seen as advisers rather than salesmen. They are ideally placed to point out how just one major repair could recoup the cost of the extended warranty.

The guide should include information on overcoming customers' objections and improving product knowledge.

> One of the problems customers and dealers face is a misunderstanding of the scope of the programme... hold a regular quiz to test knowledge of the parts covered by the warranty.

Give guidelines on operating the programme

This is perhaps the most important section of the guide. Unless everyone understands the scope of the programme, there can be misunderstandings and problems. This section should cover all the implications of the programme and should give practical guidelines on operating it. For example, it should explain all the benefits of the programme to customers and clearly state any conditions that have to be met.

The parts covered by the warranty are ... There are a number of exclusions to this list and it is important that customers and service staff understand them. Misunderstandings can lead to dissatisfied customers and wasted effort in carrying out repairs and processing claims.

Detailed instructions for operation and administration should be expressed as simply as possible and essential information highlighted.

The warranty manual sets out the procedures for operating the programme. The essential stages are ...

Summary

Retailers don't necessarily have to participate in manufacturers' business development programmes so the copy has to persuade them that participation is good for business. It also has to provide them with practical guidelines on operating the programme and selling the benefits to their customers. The programme guide must cover essential information such as:

- Describe the programme so that retailers understand what they are expected to do and how it will affect their business.

- Explain how the programme will benefit the retailers' customers; this will persuade the retailer that the programme will be easy to sell.

- Show how the programme benefits the retailer. A programme like this must offer real tangible benefits to the retailer's business.

- Provide guidelines on selling the programme so that the retailer can make the most of it. Include information on the promotional support available.

- Give guidelines on operating the programme. Administrative information should be clear and simple so that retailers do not perceive the programme as complex.

Chapter
FOURTEEN

WRITING ABOUT COMPANIES

●●

Customers don't just buy on the basis of product benefits; they may be equally concerned about the ability of a company to provide a reliable quality service. Your task is to build confidence in customers, investors and staff by explaining the company's resources and direction in the following ways:

- Demonstrating company capability.
- Demonstrating service capability.
- Repositioning a company to enter new markets.
- Recruiting good people.
- Building confidence in investors.
- Explaining a changing business to investors.

DEMONSTRATING COMPANY CAPABILITY

In many buying situations, it is important to reassure customers that they are dealing with a successful stable company. If they are going to place substantial orders, they need to know that the company will provide them with the right quality and will be able to maintain regular, reliable deliveries. The same principles apply to consumer products. A consumer who buys an expensive product needs to know that he will be able to get spare parts well into the future. When retailers are considering stocking a new brand, they want to know that the product represents quality and will not have an adverse effect on their business.

Reassure customers that they have made the right choice

> Choccibar is a new product from the Chocolate Corporation; it has continued to sell well since its launch in the American market and it has achieved brand leadership in four European countries. We have the manufacturing capability and the marketing expertise to support a successful launch in this country.

This tells the retailer that he will be taking part in a marketing success and that his own market share will prosper as a result of that involvement.

> When you buy one of our cars you're buying peace of mind because you'll get years of carefree reliable motoring, but if you ever need help, you'll find we've got a network of highly trained dealers conveniently located around the country to provide you with a rapid efficient service, wherever you are.

This tells the customer that he is not dealing with a small local organization that cannot provide reasonable back-up – the copy provides reassurance that help is at hand.

Capability is relative

Sometimes size and success are not the factors customers are looking for; small companies demonstrate a different kind of capability.

> Unlike the national giants, we prefer to offer a personal friendly service. We're small enough to care for our customers, but we have the backing of our associates to ensure that you get the right quality of service.

Big enough to be professional, but small enough to care is a familiar cry but it actually means a lot to certain types of customer. Sometimes, however, only the biggest players can succeed.

> Few companies can put together the unrivalled team that we can. As the European market leader and one of the world's largest manufacturers, we have the technical and research resources to handle a project of this complexity.

In other words, don't even think about going to a small player, this project is only for big league players.

The importance of experience is also relative. Some customers like to know that they are dealing with an established and capable supplier.

> We have been supplying customers with quality tobacco for over 200 years and we believe in maintaining a quality reputation.

This is the reassurance of a solid company. But it doesn't always appeal. Contrast the following:

> We're innovative and hungry for success. We don't have preconceived ideas and we treat every project as a challenge. If you're looking for excellence and creative thinking, we're committed.

This company suggests danger and risk but it may be worthwhile dealing with them if it achieves the right results.

Provide evidence of capability

Capability must be substantiated. It's no good saying you're the best unless you can prove it.

> We're now rated as Europe's largest service operation – we've achieved that by having a highly trained workforce in every country, running one of the biggest technical training programmes in the world and investing millions of dollars in an international service infrastructure that gives you rapid access to our global skills wherever you are in the world.

This spells out the standard of service in hard facts. If the customer wants to make a comparison, he only has to check the facts on the rivals. Prospective customers want to compare like with like when they are going through the selection process.

> We've got seventeen factories in three countries and research labs in four different centres. Our technical field force is 200 strong and we provide cover on a national basis. In the last six months we have handled a million calls and dealt satisfactorily with 85 per cent of those within a target time.

Make sure customers are aware of your capability

Capability information can help to correct perceptions of a company and put it in contention for business that it might have missed. It is essential to let customers know all about your capability.

> We're one of the premier engineering companies and our interests span most of the key markets. For example, we are leading suppliers to the armed forces of six different countries and this gives us a unique insight into military requirements. What's more, we're deeply involved in aerospace engineering and this allows us to transfer the benefits of that technology for customers in diverse markets.

Transfer capability to different markets

Sometimes capability in one field can be used to support the launch of a new product in a different market.

> After years of supplying the professional market, we've developed a unique new camera that's ideal for general family photography. We're used to meeting the demanding standards of professionals and our products have passed the quality test with lots of awards so you can trust our products to improve your own photography.

'The one the professionals use' is a favourite technique for adding a quality label to standard products. It suggests that the amateurs' performance will improve as a result of using a different sort of equipment. 'Professional quality recording tape' suggests that the product is somehow superior because quality is associated with professional use. Endorsement by leading users is another way of stressing capability – it says if we're good enough to supply these people, we're good enough to supply the average customer.

Summary

Company capability can be an important factor in selling a product. Customers want to know that they are dealing with a reliable company that will not let them down. However, capability is a relative term and 'biggest and best' may not appeal to every customer. These are the key communications tasks:

- Reassure customers that they have made the right choice; the reliability of the supplier is an important factor in that choice.

- Capability is relative – make sure you understand the factors that customers feel are important.

- Provide evidence of capability so that your claims can be substantiated. Customers make comparisons on the basis of facts as well as reputation.

- Make sure customers are aware of your capability – use a corporate reputation to win business.

- Transfer capability to different markets. Capability in one field can be used to build a reputation in a different market.

DESCRIBING PROFESSIONAL SERVICE CAPABILITY

It is more difficult to describe service capability because services are delivered by people, and the qualities that describe them may be intangible. In certain businesses the individuality of people makes it difficult to offer a consistency of service, while in other sectors it is the individual skills that are important.

Offer consistency of service

> Wherever you are in the country, you can now get the same standard of service. We have automated much of the service process so that our technicians can use sophisticated equipment to analyse the faults – they have access to a central database to find the solution quickly and they are using quality controlled spares to carry out repairs that are guaranteed.

This explains how technology can be used to back up people and provide a standard service that needs to be delivered in the same way all over the country.

Use individual skills to deliver a unique service

Sometimes, it is not consistency but individual flair that a service organization is selling, and the more unique the talent, the more they can charge for the service.

> All of our consultants come from a background in industry. They understand your business and they know what it takes to succeed. But one thing we won't give you is standard solutions because we know that you are looking for that unique solution that will give your company the competitive edge.

This is saying, don't come to us if you want predictable solutions. In the design and advertising business the opportunity to provide unique solutions for high prices is almost par for the course.

> Our task is to show our clients just how far they can go. Sure we can provide safe grey solutions, but that's not the name of the game. We're out to grab people's attention – to stand out in a crowded marketplace.

Build trust in your customers

No standard solutions in that last example! Most customers, however, are looking for something safer – a company they can trust to deliver a satisfactory level of service.

> We are an international leader in accountancy services. Our US office is the market leader in corporate finance and our European headquarters has its finger on the pulse of international business legislation. We like to give our senior partners international experience in their formative years so that later they have the breadth of experience to bring a truly global vision to your business problems.

This says that the consultancy offers more than just experienced staff; it has the international dimension that most businesses are lacking and that is something that will benefit customers directly.

Use technology to deliver a quality service

Service businesses don't just depend on people; they need to be able to exploit technology to give themselves the edge over competitors.

> We can now tune your engine in the convenience of your own driveway, using the technology that's normally reserved for the top workshops. With our diagnostic mobile workshops, we can provide you with a superb state-of-the-art service at prices a fraction of the ones you can find in the normal garage. We'll provide you with a detailed readout which shows exactly what's going on inside your car and what we've done to put it right.

This means that customers who don't like or trust normal service stations can enjoy the convenience of home tuning for a fraction of the cost. However, the copy reassures customers that they will get the same standard of service.

Improve access to your service

Technology can also be used to support the provision of the service.

> Whatever your query just dial one number and we'll make sure you get a response from the right centre of expertise. We use remote sensors to check the faults on your system and then we compare the diagnosis with known faults on our central database. That means we now have the technology to deal with faults very rapidly and in fact we can often anticipate them before they occur so that you enjoy continuous reliable operation and you don't have to put up with irritating downtime. We also respond very rapidly to your queries and can help you simplify your own support administration by giving you a single point of contact.

Given that the content of most services is similar, the winner is likely to be the company that makes it easy for customers to buy.

Demonstrate the scale of your operations

Sometimes sheer size can be the dominating factor.

> We are Europe's largest service operation. We have over 5000 trained service staff strategically located to provide you with a rapid local service and we have the technology to deliver the the most advanced solutions.

This company aims to build confidence in its large corporate customers by saying that they have the resources to match the customer organisation and provide the level of service that is needed.

Build on your specialization

But size isn't always important. The process of unbundling, where services are split into smaller activities, favours companies who are more flexible and who are willing to provide a specialist personal service.

> We don't aim to be all things to all men – instead we concentrate on our real strength which is cleaning windows – we've invested in the right equipment for the job and we've made sure that our staff are trained to carry out the job efficiently. That way we can deliver the best possible service and concentrate on our core business.

Specialization doesn't always mean small. Larger groups have organized themselves to provide a series of small specialist task forces who concentrate on providing the individual service to the customer.

> Each of our divisions is managed by a partner with profit responsibility and supported by a staff of specialists who operate like a small business. However, the strength of our group is that we can draw on the skills and resources of other companies where we need specialist support and, of

course, we have the stability and strength of being part of a financially successful international group.

That reassures larger clients who would rather deal with a major player.

Summary

Services capability is more difficult to demonstrate than manufacturing capability because service benefits are intangible. The key communications tasks include:

- Offer consistency of service; services are delivered by people and your competitors may not have the management skills or the technological back-up to offer consistency.

- Use individual skills to deliver a unique service; personal service and unique skills can prove to be a key differentiator.

- Build trust in your customers. It is important to reassure your customers that you have the resources to provide them with the right level of service.

- Use technology to deliver a quality service. This demonstrates to customers that you are investing in quality service.

- Improve access to your service. By making it easier for customers to deal with you, they reduce the complexity of their own support task.

- Demonstrate the scale of your service. If you are a major player, use the fact to build customer confidence.

- Build on your specialization. Service customers may prefer the flexibility of dealing with different groups of specialists.

REPOSITIONING A COMPANY TO ENTER A NEW MARKET

Potential customers can be influenced by a name or an image or a reputation. If a company is planning to enter new markets, it may need to modify that perception to gain initial acceptance. Your task is to identify the target perception from research and write copy that builds the new perception.

The right perception

The British Business Finance Corporation – BBFC – sounds like a large conglomerate and that could influence potential customers. It could be a merchant bank, which might intimidate smaller companies, or it may be seen as an independent operation – too small for large corporations. BBFC's problem was that it was a combination of those things – it could provide finance to small or large companies but, more important, it backed up the financial assistance with high quality management consultancy and advice.

BBFC wanted to increase its business with smaller companies by helping them develop their business. In a brochure called 'Building Business with BBFC' they set out to achieve that.

Reflect the needs of the market

The brochure begins and ends with a message from the chairman, a common enough approach in corporate brochures and annual reports. The introduction does not begin, as some brochures do, with a list of services; instead it focuses on the customer.

> People who run businesses need different things at different times to help them achieve success. Sometimes it is the investment to start, develop or even revive their company. Often it is an experienced or objective view of a business plan. Or they may be planning an expansion or relocation in the UK or overseas. BBFC works with people in all these situations and many more.

BBFC define their market through their customers. Customers can decide whether they want to work with BBFC. That introduction targets new, growing and mature companies and it also explains that BBFC offers more than finance – something that is not obvious from the company name.

Use examples to explain company policy

The brochure continues in the best tradition of management publications with a series of case histories, beginning with a quote from a famous and successful entrepreneur who had worked with BBFC from his early days as a small business owner. The message is clear – BBFC think small.

> Entrepreneurs are not as well regarded as they should be. The country would be in a lot better shape if there were more people prepared to start up their own business and more organizations like BBFC who are prepared to back them ... Companies that are not yet established find it difficult to obtain backing. So there is a very real need for organizations like BBFC which take a rather more creative and flexible view of people with good business ideas.

The copy is appealing directly to people with initiative, but no track record, the sort of people who might have had bad experiences with banks.

Use varying examples to demonstrate flexibility

The second interview is also interesting – with a director of a Japanese bank. Japanese banks are renowned for taking a long-term view of their business relationships. The City is the opposite. British firms complain that they are forced to sacrifice long-term plans for short-term returns when they obtain finance. So what better way for BBFC to demonstrate that they too are prepared to take a long-term view.

> BBFC is an important friend in the UK. One reason why we feel such an affinity is because we too take a long-term view of our lending and have over the years seen small and medium sized companies with whom we have done business grow to become leaders in their field. Supporting companies at an early stage of their growth is important to any industrial economy.

This immediately positions BBFC in a different league.

Explain how the company differs from competitors

BBFC now turn to the ordinary manager, the person with a bright idea. They are talking directly to the target audience and they are showing why they are so different from competitors. They achieve this by concentrating on the concerns that small business owners have about traditional lenders.

> As he admits himself, John Brown lacked both the financial resources and the expertise to handle the re-financing operation on his own. What he was looking for was an adviser and investment partner. BBFC may have designed the financial package that enabled Brown and his partners to acquire executive control but in every other way he was given a free hand.

Reassure customers that the company understands their concerns

As well as positioning BBFC as a company that understands small business, the brochure also shows that they are not a demanding partner. The price to pay for financial assistance is not loss of control. Here another customer confirms that BBFC take a detached view of lending.

> The real trouble was that we couldn't afford to fund the product and we desperately needed advice on almost every aspect of the business from marketing to corporate planning. We approached a number of traditional sources for help – but with no success. In every case the reaction was the same. They all wanted to know what our contribution was before they could tell us what they were prepared to put in. BBFC response was quite different.

Demonstrate that the company can meet customers' changing needs

BBFC have established that they can work with small companies, but it is important for them to reassure customers that they understand big business, because that experience may be needed at a later stage. As the customer's business grows, they will need different types of finance. BBFC include profiles of their senior management team, showing the breadth of experience they can offer customers. These profiles add to BBFC's credibility and provide a further opportunity to clarify their role.

> We are professional risk takers who operate at the leading edge of the economy helping entrepreneurs to become fully-rounded business people. And because our team at BBFC has the necessary industrial background, we can take better decisions and assume a higher level of risk than most of our customers would be prepared to contemplate.

Summary

If a company wants to move into a new market, it must position itself as a supplier that understands the needs of the market. There are a number of important communications tasks:

- Reflect the needs of the market – customers need to know that the company understands their business.

- Use examples to explain company policy; case histories are a good way of demonstrating understanding of the market.

- Use varying examples to demonstrate flexibility. This is essential if the market is diverse.

- Explain how the company differs from competitors. This helps to achieve the right positioning.

- Reassure customers that the company understands their concerns; research will identify factors that customers feel are most important.

- Demonstrate that the company can meet customers' changing needs. This helps to position the company as a long-term business partner.

RECRUITING GOOD PEOPLE

At first sight, recruitment brochures might seem to be outside the scope of marketing copy but they are important to a company's success. Unless a company can recruit and retain good people, it is unlikely to achieve its business objectives. Your task is to position the company as an employer offering opportunities for career development.

Demonstrate a commitment to people care

People are the key to business success and many companies are introducing a people care policy that encourages and helps people make their optimum contribution to the business. Although a people care policy aims to encourage staff loyalty by offering excellent employment, training and personal development, the benefit for the company is a committed, loyal workforce that can provide the highest levels of customer service and achieve quality in every aspect of the business. Better product knowledge, greater understanding of the company's aims, understanding of customer care and a desire to win, as well as the flexibility to change are the hallmarks of a company that has got its people care policies right.

This commitment to people care begins at the recruitment stage so a recruitment brochure deserves the right level of copywriting skills.

> From the moment you arrive you'll become part of a people-focused company. Every one of our employees has been through a quality course, which means we are now employing some of the best people in the business. That shows in our business performance – we're the envy of our competitors and our approach to quality serves as a model for the rest of the industry. We've also been awarded a national training award for three years as a result of this quality programme and we're now providing an external training service to other companies. We don't just concentrate on general training – we've developed a broad programme of career-based training and you'll be working closely with a career adviser who is responsible for your individual personal development. Your degree is just the starting point for your professional development.

Tell people about the company

The problem is that most recruitment folders say something along those lines – a company has to substantiate these claims and give itself a competitive edge in the recruitment market. A company profile is essential to let the recruit know what the company does and where it is going.

> We are part of an international engineering group and the market leader in our chosen sector. We've achieved this through a programme of intensive training and career development and a deliberate policy of giving early responsibility to key people. We now have plans to attack key international markets on a selective basis and our aim is to achieve market leadership through excellence in each one. This approach means that graduates will be able to achieve management responsibility even earlier and that people on the technical side will be making products that are vital to our future success immediately.

This says very clearly that people matter and that they are crucial to the company's success. It also highlights the company's plans and says that new recruits will have an important role to play – they will not just be waiting to fill other peoples' shoes. It tells technical people that they will be carrying out work that is really relevant to business success – they will not be doing research in isolation.

Create a challenge for employees

It is the element of challenge that can make the difference in attracting the right people. Industry has traditionally been seen as a last resort for graduates and the work is not regarded as stimulating. So it is important to demonstrate the challenge.

> We're currently working on some of the most advanced products in the business. For example, the RST is widely regarded as the leading laser in its field and it was developed by a team of young graduates working closely with a university research faculty. We're also introducing a quality programme which will ensure that our manufacturing operations set new industry standards. That takes effective management and, once again, our graduate teams are in the fore.

Demonstrate personal achievement

It's important to tell people they won't be in a backwater – they will get all the help they need to push their careers to the limit. The opportunity to demonstrate this is in the profiles of people who have already worked in the company and are recent graduates.

> Jane was a chemistry graduate from Nottingham who entered the research department in 1989. She worked in the fast lane programme for graduates, taking on project management at an early stage. She also attended a series of lectures at university on advanced industrial chemistry and has used this to develop a programme for our new M25 laser. As well as working on projects that are targeted at market leadership within two years, Jane is also carrying out fundamental research into the principles of propulsion and this is helping towards her PhD.

How many graduates could resist that sort of opportunity?

Summary

Recruitment literature is part of the wider discipline of employee communications. Its role is to attract good people to a company and to explain how they can contribute to the company's success. Key copy content includes:

- Demonstrate a commitment to people care by explaining how the company trains and rewards people.
- Tell people about the company so that they understand where it is going.
- Create a challenge for employees to ensure they feel they will have opportunities for personal development.
- Demonstrate personal achievement so that people can see how others have developed their careers.

BUILDING CONFIDENCE IN INVESTORS

Financial reporting presents an unusual writing challenge. Copywriters don't normally get involved with the detail of financial reporting – the profit and loss accounts and the other figures that occupy a large proportion of the annual report and accounts. They are responsible for the introductory material – the Chairman's statement and review of activities that allow the company to explain its financial performance over the last year and demonstrate how it is likely to improve its business performance over the coming financial year.

This information is important because investors and their advisers use it to make decisions about the buying and selling of shares. While this is not the only basis for decisions, it is an important one and investors pay a great deal of attention to it.

Position the company clearly

Before the report gets into the detail of the reviews and statements, it is important to remind investors what the company's business is:

> Today we remain a company whose business is investment. We have the distinctive blend of financial and industrial skills to evaluate the investment opportunities in our market sector ... We are long-term investors and have held investments in some of these companies for many years. Because we raise and invest our own funds we are extremely flexible ... What characterizes us is the way we do business. We work with people to develop imaginative responses to business opportunities and share the risks in realizing them.

This explains both what the company does and also some of the characteristics that make it successful and different from competitors. This is valuable because investors are professionals who understand balance sheets, but may not have the industrial or business experience to understand the nature of a company.

Present problems as opportunities

The Chairman's Statement gives a very general review of the company's performance in the light of current economic and business conditions. As this book was written during a period of recession, many of the current annual reports reflect the effect of those conditions.

> It was a year in which few companies if any in the financial services area were able to wholly insulate themselves against the effects of a recession which is still continuing. Difficulties, however, present a challenge and an opportunity, both of which we are now well equipped to meet. Recessionary forces have meant that in many companies there has been some refocusing on core activities. Our revised strategy, which involves discontinuing some activities

and restructuring others... Our clearer marketing positioning appears to have been well received in both UK and international markets.

Show that the business has a clear direction

It is this kind of high level review of activities that characterizes the Chairman's Statement – it sets the scene for the detailed review of activities that follows. This should pick up the main themes of the chairman's review and provide a more detailed review of performance.

> We are now pursuing a policy of concentrating on our core business: the provision of long-term investment capital to companies of all sizes without access to capital markets. During the year we have discontinued the non-core activity of management consultancy and we are running down our property development business. Despite the severe recession, net income held up well. A prudent view of some of our investments has led us to make a net provisions charge against the possibility of bad debt ... It has been our policy to adopt the same focus in our international markets ... we aim to achieve a significant position in our market sectors.

Explain the opportunities for growth

Despite the recession, the company is able to keep the confidence of its investors high.

> We have been developing our international presence over recent years ... Overall we believe there are strong indications that independent businesses are seeking the kind of investment that we offer ... Whilst expansion in the short term will be concentrated in certain countries, we remain alert to other opportunities such as those likely to arise in the longer term in eastern and central Europe. Investing risk capital abroad requires skill and experience. By training our international staff initially in the UK they are able to be effective in the field quickly.

This is ending on an upbeat note and reassuring investors that, despite the current problems, the company is well placed to take advantage of any upturn in business.

> The opportunities for our company continue to be very great indeed. The group has a clear sense of purpose and direction. Our aim is to establish the company as the leading international investment capital brand in terms of quality and creativity.

Demonstrate sound management

A later section looks at different aspects of the company's operations and presents a picture of a well-managed responsive organization that is likely to provide good growth and profit prospects in normal business conditions.

The spread of our investments by size and sector has been as varied as in any previous year. As always we have concentrated on supporting good managers in sound enterprises rather than preferred sectors or types of investment ... The profitability of the companies in our portfolio is key to our successful growth. We shall continue to place emphasis on the management of our portfolio to protect and enhance our investments.

Our relative size and our concentration on our core business means we can achieve efficient investment administration. Our new computer system is a further step towards meeting this objective ... we expect to improve our speed of response to customers and establish a lower cost base irrespective of volume.

Summary

This background information helps investors get a better understanding of the company's business and the challenges it faces. This information can be reassuring if current financial performance is poor and it can help companies when they are seeking to raise new funds or improve their share price. Key content includes:

- Position the company clearly by explaining its business and key activities.
- Present problems as opportunities by showing the actions the company is taking to overcome them.
- Show that the business has a clear direction – investors need to be aware of future prospects as well as current performance.
- Explain the opportunities for growth by describing the actions the company is taking to succeed in new markets.
- Demonstrate sound management so that investors feel confident the company can achieve the objectives it has set.

EXPLAINING A CHANGING BUSINESS TO INVESTORS

When a business changes it can put out confusing signals to many different audiences – customers, investors, suppliers and its own staff. It is vital that the company explains clearly why it is changing, where it is going and how the change will benefit each member of the audience. Your task is to write copy that will explain the nature of the change and demonstrate that it will provide significant long-term benefits.

Setting objectives

When the regional electricity boards were privatized they changed their role from being part of a State-owned distribution operation into independent service businesses that would compete with each other and new market entrants for customers previously tied by a monopoly.

In a situation like this, the Annual Report and accounts form an important part of an investor communications strategy and they have a number of key objectives.

Maintain effective investor relations
The Annual Report is part of a wider process of corporate communications and should be used to explain clearly the company's achievements and changing direction.

Position the electricity company as a dynamic well-managed business
Management skills are crucial to the electricity company's transition to an efficient, profitable independent business.

Explain the investment strategy for long-term success
It is important to explain the company's long-term direction and the steps it is taking to succeed.

Identify the concerns of the audience

Although the primary audience for an annual report is investors, it is also important to reach other people who can influence the success of the business. These include:

- existing investors – private and institutional;
- analysts;
- fund managers;
- financial advisers;
- media;
- important business clients;
- employees;
- consumer and trade associations;
- central and local government officials;
- electricity industry regulatory bodies.

Although each of these groups has individual concerns, it is possible to identify a number of key messages that would be important to all of them:

- successful transition to independent company;

- successful flotation;
- good first-year performance;
- clear direction and strategy for growth;
- strong growth prospects in core business;
- management skills to achieve business objectives;
- effective financial control;
- staff committed to highest standards of customer service;
- quality processes in place;
- ability to deliver measurable quality solutions;
- achieving operational efficiency targets;
- partnership with commercial customers.

Explain the company's key skills

One of the most important concerns of the audience will be how well the company is managing the transition to a service business. If it is to succeed, the company must demonstrate that it has the following attributes:

- investment in people;
- focused management skills;
- long-range business strategies;
- partnership with customers;
- quality improvements;
- high standards of customer service.

Demonstrate management capability

Since customers now have a choice of suppliers, the company has to demonstrate that it is capable of running an accountable, efficient business. Much of the focus in the Annual Report is on the quality of management because this is an area where nationalized industries are most strongly criticized.

> With our structure, strategy and style we aim to become a customer-oriented, people managing, problem solving organization. The new management structure is now in place and the process of changing the style in which we manage the business is gathering momentum.

In some management disciplines, the company recognizes the need to bring in outside expertise.

> Our experienced financial managers are adapting to the new accounting requirements. However, to meet the needs of the future we are introducing managerial expertise from outside the electricity supply industry in treasury, taxation and company secretarial activities. This, combined with the experience of our existing staff, is proving to be a good blend that will help us meet the challenge of the future.

Improve customer service

Improving customer service is also high on the list of essential achievements. Here the company gives a concrete example of the change.

> The shops are important points of contact with our customers for account payment, enquiries, advice and general customer service. High speed on-line communications link terminals at the shops and offices to the central computer for access to customer records. This helps us to provide a rapid customer service.

Customer service is now an integral part of the company philosophy.

> We all benefit from the process of change but we must ensure that above all the customer will gain.

Demonstrate a commitment to quality

The personnel director supports the new philosophy with a message about the relationship between customer service and quality.

> Perhaps the most significant initiative is the introduction of the Quality Improvement Programme. Its aim is to develop a high standard of service to customers in all our business relationships, both internal and external – through an ongoing commitment to improve quality and efficiency, increased personal responsibility for the standard of performance of the job, and developing a customer focused approach to all we do.

Explain the benefits of long-term partnership

Customer service plays an even stronger role in business-to-business markets where partnership is the key term.

> The relationship between the group and its customers in industry and commerce is one of partnership to try to ensure business success for our region. Showcases for this successful co-operation are the annual awards scheme for energy efficiency, whose entrants saved an estimated £4 million in energy and production costs since their inception in 1984. Industrial and commercial sales engineers are involved directly with many of the entries in

these award schemes so aiming to help improve competitive edge and reduce costs for the region's business customers.

If the company can build this type of long-term relationship with customers, the business will have a firm base and investors can look forward to continued stability.

Summary

A company that has moved from the nationalized sector into a competitive market-place must demonstrate that it has the skills, resources and commitment to succeed. Investors need to understand the actions the company has to take and they must demonstrate that they are achieving results. The annual report and accounts must meet a number of key objectives:

- Identify the concerns of the audience. Use research to identify the current perception of the company.
- Explain the key skills that will help the company to succeed in the new environment.
- Demonstrate management capability. This is perceived as a major weakness of nationalized industries.
- Improve customer service – a key factor in the company's success.
- Demonstrate commitment to quality in a practical way.
- Explain the benefits of long-term partnership. This will show investors that the company has a stable future.

INDEX

adding value 99–101
approaches to writing 19–20
auditing copy 56–9

benefits, communicating 37, 38
branding 101–5
briefing writers 12, 86–90
business issues 12
business objectives 27, 86

capability, communicating 131–7
catalogues, writing 21
change, communicating 30, 145
communications objectives 28–30, 89
communications tasks 27–30
contents list, using 81–2
copy content 81–5
   new manufacturing concept 83–4
   new model brochure 82–3
   new service 84–5
   sales presentation 82
corporate brochures, writing 25–6
customer expectations, reflecting 47, 50
customer care, communicating 28, 29, 61–4, 65, 124–7

data sheets, writing 22
dealer communications 25, 124–7, 128–30
decision makers 31–40, 46, 47, 69–71, 74–5, 77–8
   board members 33–4
   project teams 34–8
   purchasing managers 32, 33
   senior management 39
   technical managers 33
   trainees 40
   training managers 39, 40

executive brochures, writing 23–4

financial communications 143–9

importance of copywriting 17–19
internal communications 49, 52, 58–9

key messages, developing 67–80
   accountancy services 72–3
   computers 68–71
   credit cards 73–4
   furniture 71–2
   industrial materials 77–8
   lawn mowers 67–8
   leisure centres 76–7
   telephones 78–9
   training services 74–5
   video cameras 75–6

language of copywriting 60–6
   customer care 61–4
   quality 60–1
   technology 64–6
leaflets, writing 20–1

management guides, writing 23
market segmentation 115–17
marketing communications 11
marketing objectives 27, 86–7

new market development 112–15, 117–24
new product launch 35, 43–4, 93–9

partnership, communicating 29, 30, 62–3, 148–9

perceptions
    changing 50–2
    customer 50
    internal 49, 52
perceptions, planning 48–55, 88, 137
    airline 53
    bank mortgages 54
    builders 53
    pasta 52, 53
    petrol 55
    sports and leisure 54
positioning 137–40, 143
product brochures, writing 21–2
product guides, writing 22
purchasing factors 47
purchasing situations 40–4

quality, communicating 12, 60–1

research 12, 46–7, 48, 49

sales guides, writing 24
salesforce communications 24–5, 122–4
scope of copywriting 17–26

target audience 31–45, 64–5, 87–8, 89–90
    analysing 31, 38–40
    concerns 36
technical update, writing 23
technology, communicating 64–6, 68–71, 96–9, 105–8
training, communicating 28, 38–40, 74–5, 108–11